CRIMINAL ABORTION:

ITS NATURE, ITS EVIDENCE, AND ITS LAW.

By HORATIO R. STORER, M.D., LL.B.,

FELLOW OF THE AMERICAN ACADEMY OF ARTS AND SCIENCES, AND LATE PROFESSOR OF OBSTETRICS AND MEDICAL JURISPRUDENCE IN BERKSHIRE MEDICAL COLLEGE;

AND

FRANKLIN FISKE HEARD.

THE LAWBOOK EXCHANGE, LTD.
Clark, New Jersey

ISBN 9781584777670 (hardcover)
ISBN 9781616192679 (paperback)

Lawbook Exchange edition 2008, 2012

The quality of this reprint is equivalent to the quality of the original work.

THE LAWBOOK EXCHANGE, LTD.
33 Terminal Avenue
Clark, New Jersey 07066-1321

Please see our website for a selection of our other publications and fine facsimile reprints of classic works of legal history:
www.lawbookexchange.com

Library of Congress Cataloging-in-Publication Data

Storer, Horatio Robinson, 1830-1922.
Criminal abortion : its nature, its evidence, and its law / Horatio R. Storer and Franklin
Fiske Heard.
p. cm.
Reprint. Originally published: Boston : Little, Brown, 1868.
Includes bibliographical references.
ISBN-13: 978-1-58477-767-0 (cloth : alk. paper)
ISBN-10: 1-58477-767-2 (cloth : alk. paper)
1. Abortion. I. Heard, Franklin Fiske, 1825-1889. II. Title.
RA1067S86 2007
363.46--dc22
2006035840

Printed in the United States of America on acid-free paper

CRIMINAL ABORTION:

ITS NATURE, ITS EVIDENCE, AND ITS LAW.

By HORATIO R. STORER, M.D., LL.B.,

FELLOW OF THE AMERICAN ACADEMY OF ARTS AND SCIENCES, AND LATE PROFESSOR OF OBSTETRICS AND MEDICAL JURISPRUDENCE IN BERKSHIRE MEDICAL COLLEGE;

AND

FRANKLIN FISKE HEARD.

BOSTON:

LITTLE, BROWN, AND COMPANY.

1868.

CAMBRIDGE:
PRESS OF JOHN WILSON AND SON.

TO

THOSE WHOM IT MAY CONCERN,

COUNSELLOR, JUROR, JUDGE, AND PHSYICIAN,

THESE PAGES

ARE RESPECTFULLY INSCRIBED.

PREFACE.

Lawyers and physicians should stand to each other, in medico-legal matters, as associates working together for the common good of society, rather than as adversaries liable to be thought endeavoring to make the worse appear the better reason. The crime of unjustifiable abortion is now recognized by both the professions as of frequent occurrence, and as going too often unwhipt of justice. Certain papers upon the subject, first published in the "North-American Medico-Chirurgical Review," at Philadelphia, during the year 1859, and then re-issued from the press in a collective form, have done somewhat to uncover the crime, and perhaps, what is better, to prevent it. Argumentation, however, though cogent, and ethics, though divine, are insufficient, this side of eternity, to restrain the vices and passions of mankind.

The signs of the times lead us to believe that the publication of this book, which is in part re-written from that above referred to, will be no premature delivery. Nine long years have passed since the idea upon which it is based was first conceived, — a time that even the proverbial slowness of the law will allow to be a full and sufficient term of gestation. In acting as its accoucheurs, we not merely hope for it success in the world upon its own merits; but in view of the great interests, legal, moral, and religious, that it will tend, we trust, to subserve, we have carried still further the not wholly inappropriate simile; and, though this symbol is rather an unusual one for a law-book, we have marked its face with the sign of the cross.

In writing that portion which treats of the Criminal Law, it has been the aim of the authors to exhaust the subject. The cases have been stated so fully as to preclude the necessity of examining the volumes of Reports from which they are taken. This has been done not only for the benefit of the non-professional reader, but for the reason that many of the cases cited are taken from English Reports, which are not generally accessible, even to the legal Profession, in this country. Free use has been made of the fifth edition of "RUSSELL on Crimes," London, 1865. This edition, edited by Mr. GREAVES, for accuracy and completeness is not surpassed by any text-book in the law.

The practitioner in the criminal courts, whether engaged in the prosecution or defence, will find Precedents of Indictments, — many of which have been drawn expressly for this work, — and the evidence necessary to support them.

H. R. S.
F. F. H.

BOSTON, August, 1868.

TABLE OF CONTENTS.

BOOK I.

FROM THE STAND-POINT OF MEDICINE.

BOOK II.

FROM THE STAND-POINT OF LAW.

CRIMINAL ABORTION.

BOOK I.

FROM THE STAND-POINT OF MEDICINE.

CHAPTER I.

IS ABORTION EVER A CRIME?

At the Common Law, and by many of our State codes, fœtal life, per se, is almost wholly ignored, and its destruction unpunished; abortion, in every case, being considered an offence mainly against the mother, and as such, unless fatal to her, a mere misdemeanor, or wholly disregarded.

By the Moral Law, THE WILFUL KILLING OF A HUMAN BEING AT ANY STAGE OF ITS EXISTENCE IS MURDER.

In undertaking the discussion of this subject, three preliminary facts must be assumed: —

First. — That, if abortion be ever a crime, it is of necessity, even in isolated cases, one of no small interest to moralist, jurist, and physician; and that, when general and common, this interest is extended to the whole community, and fearfully enhanced.

Secondly. — That, if the latter assumption be true, both in premise and conclusion, — neglected as the crime has been by most ethical writers and political economists, hastily passed over by medical jurists,[1] and confessedly everywhere the great opprobrium of the law, often indeed by taunt that of medicine, — either it cannot in the nature of things be suppressed, as by these facts implied, or its suppression has not been properly attempted. Discarding the former of these alternatives, as alike unworthy of belief, and proved false by facts hereafter to be shown, it will appear, —

Thirdly. — That the discussion now broached is neither supererogatory nor out of place; further, that it is absolutely and necessarily demanded.

Moreover, in order that the importance and various bearings of the subject may be better appreciated, and that the writer's position and aims may be more fairly understood, it must be borne in mind that there exist to this discussion certain positive and apparent objections, which have, in a measure, given rise to much of the silence and omission alluded to above, and are, in the main, as follows: —

1. The natural dislike of any physician to enter upon a

[1] So far as the writer is aware, there existed, neither in this nor any other language, at the time he first commenced its consideration, any paper upon the subject, at all commensurate with its importance. The chapters devoted to it in medical text-books, though some of them, especially that of Beck, admirable so far as they went, were defective and often erroneous; while but little information of any value could be found elsewhere. In the French periodicals there had appeared articles on special points hereafter referred to; in Great Britain, able arguments regarding the commencement of fœtal life had been made by RADFORD (1848); and in this country, with remarks on the frequency of the crime, by HODGE, of Philadelphia (1839 and 1854), and, in 1855, by the present Professor of Obstetrics in Harvard University. To the latter, his father, and to the journalists (MORLAND and MINOT, of Boston), by whom the effort then made was so warmly and eloquently seconded, the writer acknowledged, at the time, his indebtedness for the thought of the undertaking, which has culminated, he has reason to believe, in an agitation which is now shaking society, throughout our country, to its very centre.

Eight years have now passed. Not only has the medical profession been stirred to progressive action; but, through its members, the outside community. Paper after paper upon the subject has been issued by medical men; the religious press has become deeply interested; political economists have found, as had been indicated in the previous edition of this book, an explanation of otherwise inexplicable problems; an impetus of the most powerful

subject, on some points of which it is probable that a portion of his own profession is at variance with him, either from disbelief in the alleged increase of criminal abortion, unnoticed for reasons shown hereafter, or from a blind reliance on Providence of itself to abate the evil.

2. His fear, lest by any possible chance, by showing the frequency of the crime and its means, he may unhappily cause its still further increase.

3. The reluctance on the part of many of his profession to attack a powerful and acknowledged moneyed interest;

4. And to tell their patients, more commonly than is yet general, most unwelcome truth; thus not merely condemning, but, to their own consciences at least, criminating them;

5. And individually to risk losing practice, if thought more scrupulous than others;

6. And to be brought into more frequent contact with the law, even though for ends of justice;

character has been given to the movement, by the publication, under the auspices of the American Medical Association, of the author's two books for the people, entitled "Why Not? a Book for Every Woman," and "Is It I? a Book for Every Man;" and we find one of the ablest and most conservative of the theological writers of the present day, the Rev. Dr. JOHN TODD, with his "Woman's Rights, a Plea for a Holier Living," confronted by as able and as fearless a writer of the other sex, "GAIL HAMILTON," with her "Woman's Wrongs, a Counter-irritant," in which, however covertly, the idea is practically upheld, that, whatever her other rights, a woman is certainly entitled to decide whether or no she shall bear children. The importance of the subject is rapidly becoming recognized by the legal as well as by the medical profession; and extracts from the author's writings upon the subject, presented through the pages of ELWELL's treatise on Malpractice and Medical Evidence, and the later American editions of TAYLOR's Medical Jurisprudence, have already affected the rulings of courts. The early exhaustion of the previous edition of this book, which has long been out of print, and the fact that its writer has frequently been consulted in these matters by criminal lawyers, cause him to trust that the present edition, in the preparation of the first portion of which he has had valuable aid from his assistant in practice, Dr. ALEXANDER J. STONE, while the latter half is wholly due to his accomplished colleague, Mr. HEARD, may secure the approval of the two great bodies of professional men for whom as a manual it has been written.

7. And to exercise greater care and discretion in diagnosis and treatment, lest themselves be brought to answer for malpractice, or worse;

8. And publicly to discuss matters supposed to be generally unknown, and thus seem to throw open professional secrets to the world.

9. And, finally, grave doubts lest the statements made, though simple and true, should yet appear so astounding as to shock belief, or so degrading as to tend to lessen all faith in natural affection and general morality.

But these objections, so far at least as regards the medical profession, are undoubtedly but of limited existence; and, on the other hand, as more than counterbalancing them all, are the following arguments: —

That medical men are the physical guardians of women and their offspring; from their position and peculiar knowledge necessitated in all obstetric matters to regulate public sentiment, and to govern the tribunals of justice.

That the discussion by them of this crime may very probably be the means, in great measure, of ultimately restraining or suppressing its perpetration.

That such will undoubtedly tend to save much health to the community, and many human lives.

And that, were there no other reason, it is clearly a duty.

We shall accordingly proceed to prove, so far as possible, the truth of every premise as yet stated, and to show the real nature and frequency of the crime; its causes; its victims; its perpetrators and its innocent abettors; its means and its proofs; its excuses, the deficiencies and errors, on medico-legal points, of existing laws, and the various other obstacles to conviction; and, above all, the duty of the medical and legal professions toward its general suppression. We shall endeavor to present the matter as succinctly as is possible consistently with its extent, its novelty, and its importance.

That the true nature of an unjustifiable and criminal abortion could have been doubted, least of all by mothers, however ignorant or degraded, would at first sight appear improbable. The sense of the public, however, its practice, its laws, being each proved fatally erroneous by the stubborn evidence of facts, the necessity of our preliminary inquiry will be made manifest.

To postpone, for the present, all other considerations, we will regard abortion in the abstract. It may be defined best, perhaps, as the violent and premature expulsion of the product of conception, independently of its age, viability, and normal formation.[1] These characteristics are eliminated as having judicially and actually nothing to do with the essential nature of abortion, whereas in infanticide they are each elements of great importance; a difference that will hereafter be seen.

We further, in the present investigation, set aside all cases where abortion is the result of accident, or from natural causes,[2] or justified by the rules of medicine, whether to save the mother or her child. We shall have occasion, in the subsequent course of our inquiries, to discuss this latter question somewhat fully, and to set forth unpleasant truths. We now confine ourselves exclusively to those instances where the attempt at premature expulsion of the product of conception is artificially induced and intentional, and where, so far as can be judged,

1 We are well aware that legal, as well as many medical writers, have restricted the term abortion to instances of delivery previous to the seventh month of gestation, this being considered the earliest period of the so-called viability of the child. The distinction is, however, a forced and unnatural one: viability is possible before the period alluded to; the technical infanticide cannot be committed until the fœtus has been wholly born; and it would be very wrong, were its unjustifiably intentional expulsion during the last three months of pregnancy to be, or to seem, uncovered by the law.

2 We have elsewhere given some attention to the above points; as in a paper entitled "Studies of Abortion," contained in the Boston Medical and Surgical Journal for February, 1863.

it is not necessitated, and would not otherwise have occurred.

In the first place, the laws do not recognize that unnecessary abortion, intrinsically considered, is a crime.

This act, when unnecessarily done, must be for one of two reasons, — either to prevent the product of conception from receiving life, which subsequent evidence will show cannot be the case, or, if living, to destroy it.

We have said that the common law and many of our American statutes lose sight of this fundamental idea. Though based upon the first of the above alternatives, — the erroneous one, as regards the fact of their existence, — they are so worded as almost wholly to ignore fœtal life, to refuse it protection, to insure their own evasion, and by their inherent contradictions to extend the very crime they were framed to prevent.

They recognize, for the most part, no offence against the fœtus; we have just shown that such, and such alone, is always intended. They punish an attempt, which does not exist, upon the well-being or life of the mother; the intent being seldom or never to destroy the parent. She is herself, in almost every case, a party to the action performed; an accessory or the principal. To constitute a crime, a malicious or wicked intent is supposed to exist; we have thrown aside, as does the law, every case occurring from accident or from justifiable cause. The intent, if existing, as of course must be always the case, is against, and only against, the product of conception.

Again, the punishment meted by the law proves the truth of these propositions. Unless the woman die in consequence of the offence, it is declared, in every stage of pregnancy, a mere misdemeanor; or else, while called such, or by omission justified or openly allowed, in the early months when the fœtus is without other safeguard, the law pronounces abortion a felony and increases its penalties in more advanced pregnancy, after quickening has rendered it infinitely more certain that the fœtus will remain undisturbed, and has thus in a great majority of cases prevented the crime.

On the other hand, granting for the moment that the erroneous assumptions of the law were correct, and that the attempt were upon the life of the mother, how inconsistent to punish murder, attempted or committed, if by injury to the throat or heart, capitally, and, if by injury to the womb, by temporary imprisonment! especially where this latter case always necessitates the slaughter of a second human victim.

Or, granting that the attempt were only upon the mother's health or temporary welfare, how absurd to punish the offence in early pregnancy, where her risks are greatest, by a trifling penalty or not at all, and in more advanced pregnancy, where these risks are daily lessened, with increased severity!

And finally, if the fœtus were, as has been sometimes supposed, merely *pars viscerum matris*, its removal would be like that of a limb, or of any other portion of the body, whose loss is not necessarily attended with that of life. If made with the mother's consent, the act would be unpunishable by law; if against her will, it would be already amenable, like other maim or mutilation, to existing statutes. In the one case, laws against abortion were needless; in the other, unjustifiable.

In a word, then, in the sight of the common law, and in most cases of the statutory law also, the crime of abortion, properly considered, does not exist; the law discussing and punishing a wholly supposititious offence, which not only does not exist, but the very idea of whose existence is simply absurd.

We turn now to public opinion. It, too, both in theory and in practice, fails to recognize the crime. Its practical denial of the true character of the offence will be shown in the course of our remarks on its frequency. Its theoretical denial we here consider as proved in three ways, — by implication, by collateral testimony, and by direct.

First, the maxims of the law are based on past or present public opinion. If merely on past, and this has totally changed, the law, in matters of such importance, is compelled to change also. The fact that the laws on this subject remain unaltered, — if it be granted, as we have asserted, and as will be proved, that they are erroneous, — furnishes us, at the outset and so far, with evidence that public opinion was formerly wrong, and that it so continues.

The frequency of the offence, and the character and standing of the mothers upon whose persons it is practised, accessories as we have seen, or principals to it, furnish similar and more cogent testimony regarding the theory upon which it is founded. We shall soon perceive how extensive and high-reaching is the frequency; we must therefore conclude that the public do not know, or knowing deny, the criminal character of the action performed.

Again, the direct testimony of the parties themselves is often available. It is undoubtedly a common experience, as it has certainly been that of the writer, for a physician to be assured by his patients, — often, no doubt, falsely, but frequently with sincerity, — that their abortions have been induced in utter ignorance of the commission of wrong; in the belief that the contents of the womb, so long as manifesting no perceptible sign of life, were but lifeless and inert matter: in other words, that, being, previously to quickening, a mere ovarian excretion, they might be thrown off and expelled from the system as coolly and as guiltlessly as those from the bladder and rectum.

It having now been shown, directly and by temporary assumption, that the law and public sentiment, both by their theory and their practice, alike deny to unjustifiable abortion the imputation of crime, it remains for us to discuss this question abstractly, and to prove, not merely that they are wrong, but that the offence is one of the deepest guilt, a crime SECOND TO NONE.

Ignorance of the law is held no excuse. The plea of ignorance of guilt could hardly better avail where its existence is implied by common sense, by analogy, and by all natural instinct, binding even on brutes.[1] Were this guilt, however, clearly shown, and its knowledge, supposed wanting, to be spread broadcast by the press, — the all-powerful arbiter of public opinion, — the last and strongest prop of the crime were gone.

It has been shown, by setting aside all accidental cases, — those naturally occurring and those necessarily, — and in the absence of reasonable evidence to the contrary, that all other abortions must be intentional, that they must be occasioned by the "malice aforethought" of the law. It has also been shown that in these cases, except it exist as an additional element, the malicious intention is not against the life or person of the mother; but that in every instance it is against the product of her womb. Hence, the whole question of the criminality of the offence turns on this one fact, — the real nature of the fœtus *in utero*. If the fœtus be a lifeless excretion, however soon it might have received life, the offence is comparatively as *nothing:* if the fœtus be already, and from the very outset, a human being alive, however early its stage of development, and existing independently of its mother, though drawing its sustenance from

[1] The fact that some of the lower mammals — as cats, swine, &c, — at times devour their young, is no argument to the contrary of what we have above stated. Just as obtains in a large majority of the cases of infanticide, or murder of the child after its birth, in our own species, the act is owing to an aberration of instinct, itself the result of disease; a striking illustration of reflex disturbance of the nervous centres from irritation of the uterus or ovaries, or some other organic or pelvic lesion. The wholesale destruction of the young of their own species, after they are partly grown, by animals of types still lower in the scale, — as the mackerel, for instance, among fishes, — is more rationally to be explained upon the ground of a passing-away of parental instinct with the season of parturition or spawning, than by any assumed intention, upon the part of the Creator, of furnishing political economists with a basis for Malthusian doctrines, or fashionable women with an argument for child murder, and for their own physical destruction, so often accompanying this crime.

her, the offence becomes, in every stage of pregnancy, MURDER.

"Every act of procuring abortion," rules Judge King, of Philadelphia,[1] contrary to the usual interpretation of the law, "is murder, whether the person perpetrating such act intended to kill the woman, or merely feloniously to destroy the fruit of her womb."

Common sense, we have said, would lead us to the conclusion that the fœtus is from the very outset a living and distinct being. It is alike absurd to suppose identity of bodies and independence of life, or independence of bodies and identity of life; the mother and the child within her, in abstract existence, must be entirely identical from the conception of the latter to its birth, or entirely distinct. Allowing, then, as must be done, that the ovum does not originate in the uterus; that for a time, however slight, during its passage through the Fallopian tube, its connection with the mother is wholly broken; that its subsequent history after impregnation is one merely of development, its attachment merely for nutrition and shelter,—it is not rational to suppose that its total independence, thus once established, becomes again merged into total identity, however temporary; or that life, depending not on nine months' growth, nor on birth, because confessedly existing long before the latter period,—from quickening at least, a time varying within wide limits,—dates from any other epoch than conception; while it is as irrational to think that the influence of the father, mental and moral as well as physical, so often and so plainly manifested, can be exercised by any possibility upon the child at any other moment than that original and only one of impregnation itself. We can recognize no period during uterine life, any more than in that after birth, during which the individual is more alive than at another.

Another argument is furnished us, similar, but differing.

[1] As quoted by HODGE, Introductory Lecture, Philadelphia, 1854, p. 15.

The fœtus previous to quickening, as after it, must exist in one of two states, — either death or life. The former cannot take place, nor can it ever exist, except as a finality. If its signs do not at once manifest themselves, after its occurrence, as is generally the case, and the fœtus be retained *in utero*, it must become either mummified or disintegrated: it can never again become vivified. If, therefore, death has not taken place, and we can conceive no other state of the fœtus save one, that, namely life, must exist from the beginning.

These reasonings are strengthened by the evidence of analogy. The utter loss of direct influence by the female bird upon its offspring from the time the egg has left her, and the marked effect, originally, of the male; the independence in body, in movement, and in life, of young marsupial mammals, almost from the very moment of their conception, identical analogically with the intra-uterine state of other embryos, — nourishment by teat merely replacing that by placenta at an earlier period; the same in birds, shown by movements in their egg on cold immersion before the end of incubation; the permanence of low vitality, or of impaired or distorted nervous force, arising from early arrest or error of development, and necessarily contemporaneous with it, — are all instances in point.

Brute instincts are often thought wholly supplanted by human reason. That this is not so is proved by what obtains in the absence of reason, whether from the outset or subsequently occurring. Idiots and lunatics alike show the actual identity in this respect of man and the brute,[1] how-

[1] In a work to which we have already alluded, written for the perusal of men, we have taken occasion to show, somewhat forcibly, that brutishness in one instinct, that of sexual gratification, is by no means ordinarily confined to idiots and persons considered by their fellows bereft of mind. There is no doubt that rape, such in every sense save its technical acknowledgment by the law, is frequently committed in the marriage-bed by the husband upon the sick or unwilling wife, and that this is done year after year, until death brings release. There is no doubt, again, that many cases of legal rape

ever instinct, in the former, may normally be tempered by conscience and reason. Whatever ideas on the subject of abortion the human mind may have forced itself to entertain, let the slightest proof concerning the existence of fœtal life be alleged, and maternal instinct generally at once makes itself known: the parent, as after its birth, would often even perish to preserve her child. This is not conscience, which is stirred only by an after-thought; but instinct.

Thus far incidental proof concerning the commencement of fœtal life, and so the guilt of unjustifiable abortion. More decisive evidence is at hand.

That the movements of the fœtus, subsequent to quickening, whatever the actual nature of that first sensation may be, declare the existence of intra-uterine life, is allowed by the world; by none more than by mothers themselves, whose statistics prove that, after the perception of these movements, criminal abortions are comparatively rare.

But quickening — a period usually occurring from the one hundred and fifteenth to the one hundred and thirtieth day after conception, but varying within still more appreciable limits in different women, and in the same women in different pregnancies, from variations in the amount of liquor amnii, the early strength of the fœtus, and other causes, and also, if at all owing in its first sensation to rising of the womb from the pelvis, probably occurring a little earlier with boys than with girls, from their relative difference in size[1] — is often absent, even throughout pregnancy;

are the direct result of mental disease, primarily or secondarily existing; erotomania in the male being at times as distinctly the effect of local irritation from hæmorrhoids, ascarides, urinary calculus, &c., &c., as is nymphomania in the female. There are many points in this connection of extreme interest to medical experts and to counsel, to some of which we have referred in our papers upon the Law of Rape, in the New-York Medical Journal for 1865, and the New-York Quarterly Journal of Psychological Medicine and Medical Jurisprudence for 1868.

[1] Hippocrates states that this is a fact, and that he had found the difference of a whole month, which he attributes to the "greater strength" of

and fœtal movements are sometimes appreciable to the attendant when not to the mother, or, indeed, they may be to the mother alone.

Further, in premature births where quickening has not occurred, or before its usual period, by the movement of the fœtus its earlier independent and vital existence is sometimes reduced to a matter of ocular demonstration; while to the ear, in very many instances, as early and as conclusive evidence is afforded by the sounds these movements give rise to.[1]

Quickening is therefore as unlikely a period for the commencement of fœtal life as those others set by Hippocrates and his successors, varying from the third day after conception to that of the Stoics, namely birth, and as false as them all.

We need not, with Dubois[2] and some earlier writers[3] from the manifest relation of means to the end, consider that the movements of the fœtus *in utero*, and its consequent attitude and position, are signs of an already developed and decided sentience and will; nor is it requisite to suppose them the effect of an almost rational instinct. But that they are wholly independent of the will and the consciousness of the mother, and yet by no means characteristic of organic life, whether hers or its own,—which latter is also by abundant evidence proved independently to exist,—but decidedly animal in their character; that they are not

the male. (On the Nature of the Child, sect. 11.) We are unaware that this point has been investigated by any modern writer.

1 "These sounds may sometimes be distinguished *several weeks* before the mother becomes conscious of the motions of the child."—NAEGELE, Treatise on Obstetric Auscultation, p. 50.

2 Mémoire sur la Cause des Présentations de la Tête, &c.—Mém. de l'Acad. Roy. de Méd., tome ii.

3 A. PARÉ, English Trans., p. 899. HUGH CHAMBERLEN'S Trans. of MAURICEAU on Diseases of Women with Child, p. 147, note. ENNEMOSER, Historisch-physiologische Untersuchungen über den Ursprung und das Wesen der menschlichen Seele; Bonn, 1824. CABANIS, Rapports du Physique et du Moral de l'Homme, tome ii. p. 431.

explainable by gravity, despite all the arguments alleged, as by Matthews Duncan,[1] nor on any other supposition save that of a special and independent excito-motory system, distinct from that of the mother,[2] brings us directly down to this, — the existence of as distinct and independent a nervous centre, self-existing, self-acting, living.

We set aside all the speculations of metaphysicians regarding moral accountability of the fœtus, the "potential man," and its "inanimate vitalities," as useless as they are bewildering. If there be life, then also the existence, however undeveloped, of an intellectual, moral, and spiritual nature, the inalienable attribute of humanity, is implied.

If we have proved the existence of fœtal life before quickening has taken place or can take place, and by all analogy, and a close and conclusive process of induction, its commencement at the very beginning, at conception itself, we are compelled to believe unjustifiable abortion always a crime.[3]

And now words fail. Of the mother, by consent or by her own hand, imbrued with her infant's blood; of the equally guilty father, who counsels or allows the crime; of the wretches who by their wholesale murders far out-Herod Burke and Hare; of the public sentiment which palliates, pardons, and would even praise this so common violation of all law, human and divine, of all instinct, of all reason, all pity, all mercy, all love, — we leave those to speak who can.

[1] Edinburgh Medical and Surgical Journal, Jan. 1855, p. 50.

[2] Simpson, Obstetric Works, edited by Priestley and H. R. Storer, vol. ii. p. 88.

[3] It will be noticed, that, in the medical portion of this work, no discussion is had of the technical character or evidence of infanticide, the murder of a child after its birth; whereas, in the legal portion, it is necessary incidentally to refer to it as bearing upon collateral questions. There are, however, so many points involved of importance and interest, that it is possible we may conjointly discuss this crime also, in a future publication.

CHAPTER II.

ITS FREQUENCY, AND THE CAUSES THEREOF.

THOUGH we cannot at once, and in exact figures, show the yearly amount of criminal abortion in this country, statistics on the subject being necessarily imperfect or wanting, we may yet arrive at an approximate result. This is done by an easy and reliable process of induction, the several factors of which, each of itself rendering probable the conclusion, tend, when combined, to make it almost absolutely certain.

We are to consider, in this connection, the evidence afforded by —

1. The comparative increase of population.
2. The published records of still-births.
3. The number of arrests, or trials for abortion.
4. The published number of immediate maternal deaths.
5. The pecuniary success of abortionists, and venders of abortion-producing nostrums.
6. The comparative size of families in present and past times.
7. The experience of physicians, — direct from applications for abortion and actual cases thereof, and indirect from their results.

Several of these points were, at the time we commenced our investigations, almost wholly uninvestigated. They were stated, therefore, with care, as bearing decidedly on the question at issue, and as tending to provoke still further research.

1. Let us first consider the rate of increase of our population.

To go into an elaborate comparison of our national and State censuses with themselves, past and present, with each other, and with those of similar communities abroad, involving, as it would do, intricate calculations regarding the effect of emigration from State to State and from nation to nation, the increase of urban population, and the frequent decrease of rural, was not our intention, nor was it necessary. By considering this point in connection with that immediately succeeding it, with which it is intimately related, its bearing and importance will at once be seen.

Statistics in this country were as yet so imperfect, as is indeed still the case, that we were necessitated to the logic of deduction. If it can be shown that a state of things prevails elsewhere to a certain extent, explainable only on one supposition, and that the same state of things prevails in this country to a greater extent — all other causes, save the one referred to, being in great measure absent — little doubt can be entertained of the part this plays; but if it can, in addition, be proved that this cause must necessarily be stronger with us than elsewhere, then its existence becomes morally certain. Accordingly, if we find that in another country living births are steadily lessening in proportion alike to the population and to its increase; that natural or preventive causes are insufficient to account for this, while the proportion of still-births and of known abortions is constantly increasing, and these last bear an evident yet increasing ratio to the still-births; that in this country the decrease of living births, and the increase of still-births, are in much greater ratio to the population, and the proportion of premature births is also increasing; that these relations are constant, and yearly more marked, — we are justified in supposing that abortions are at least as frequent with us as in that country, and probably more so.

I am aware that the evidence of statistics is received by many minds with a certain measure of doubt; but I shall endeavor so to add proof to proof, and to draw these from such authoritative sources, that no doubt can fairly remain. I base my remarks upon the following self-evident laws: —

1st, That, while a result or event in *individual* instances is ever variable and uncertain, this result or event, when calculated from or upon *masses* of instances, becomes proportionately certain and invariable.

2d, That, to apply this principle to the case we are now considering, the *absolute* number of *living births* in a given population in a given time should, in the absence of an evident and sufficient disturbing cause, be always nearly the same; increasing with the increase of the population, and with the progress of medical science (which might easily be proved to be in this respect constantly advancing).

3d, That the *absolute* number of *still-births at the full period of pregnancy*, occurring from natural causes in a given time in a given population, should be always nearly the same; increasing only in proportion to the actual increase of the population, and decreasing with the progress of medical science.

4th, That the *absolute* number of *premature* births, occurring from natural causes in a given time in a given population, should be always nearly the same; increasing only in proportion to the actual increase of the population, and decreasing with the progress of medical science.

5th, That the *relative* number of *still-births from natural causes*, at the full period of pregnancy and premature, as compared with the *living* births in a given population in a given time, should be always nearly the same; *not* being affected by an increase of population, and constantly lessened by the progress of medical science.

6th, That the *relative* number of *still-births from natural causes*, at the full period of pregnancy and premature, as compared with the *general mortality* in a given population in a given time, should remain always nearly the same; not being affected by an increase of population, and but slightly by the progress of medical science.

7th, That the *relative* number of *still-births from natural causes*, premature and at the full period of pregnancy, should remain always nearly the same compared with each other; neither of them being affected by the increase of population, and each of them nearly equally by the progress of medical science.[1]

In many countries of Europe, it has been ascertained that the "fecundity" of the population, or the rate of its annual increase, is rapidly diminishing.

In Sweden, it has lessened by one-ninth in 61 years; in Prussia, by a third in 132 years; in Denmark, by a quarter in 82 years; in England, by two-sevenths in a century; in Russia, by an eighth in 28 years; in Spain, by a sixth in 30 years; in Germany, by a thirteenth in 17 years; in France, by a third in 71 years.[2]

Or, in other words: —

In Sweden, it has lessened by a fifth; in Prussia, by a fourth; in Denmark and England, by a third; and in Russia, Spain, Germany, and France, by a half, — in a single century.

For the sake of convenience, larger bodies of statistics existing concerning it, and from the fact that it represents the extreme of the alleged decrease, we take France for our comparisons.

In France at large, according to the official returns as analyzed by Legoyt, the increase of the population, which from 1801 to 1806 was at the rate of 1.28 per cent annu-

[1] Many of the statistics now presented we have also embodied in a paper upon the Decrease of the Rate of Increase of Population now obtaining in Europe and America, read before the American Academy of Arts and Sciences, Dec. 14, 1858, as a contribution to the Science of Political Economy, and published in Silliman's Journal of Science and Art, New Haven, March, 1867.

[2] Moreau De Jonnés, Eléments de Statistique, 1856, p. 202.

ally, from 1806 to 1846 had fallen to about .5 per cent.[1] The exact ratio of decrease after this point is better shown by the figures themselves. The increase from 1841 to 1846 was 1,200,000; from 1846 to 1851, 380,000; from 1851 to 1856, 256,000.

In England, during this latter period, with a population of but one-half the size, the returns of the Registrar-General show a relative increase nine times greater.[2] In thirty-seven years, from 1817 to 1854, the mean annual increase in France was not more than 155,929; yet in five years, from 1846 to 1851, it had fallen to 76,000 yearly, and, from 1851 to 1856, to 51,200, and this with a population ranging from twenty-nine to thirty-four millions.

A comparison of these facts, with those obtaining in other European States, will make the above still more evident. We now quote from Rau.[3]

	Rate of increase. Per cent.
Hungary, according to Rohrer	2.40
England, from 1811 to 1821	1.78
,, from 1821 to 1831	1.60
Prussia, from 1816 to 1827	1.54
,, from 1820 to 1830	1.37
,, from 1821 to 1831	1.27
Austria (Rohrer)	1.30
Scotland, from 1821 to 1831	1.30
Netherlands, from 1821 to 1828	1.28
Saxony, from 1815 to 1830	1.15
Baden (Heunisch), from 1820 to 1830	1.13
Bavaria, from 1814 to 1828	1.08
Naples, from 1814 to 1824	0.83
France (Mathieu), from 1817 to 1827	0.63
France, more recently (De Jonnés)	0.55

A similar and corroborative table, containing additional matter, is given by Quetelet;[4] its differences from the preceding are owing to its representing a series of different years.

1 Journal des Economistes, March and May, 1847.

2 Edinburgh Review, Jan. 1857, p. 342; Med. Times and Gazette, May, 1857, p. 462.

3 Lehrbuch der Politischen Oekonomie.

4 Sur l'Homme et la Développpement de ses Facultés, tome i. ch. 7.

	Rate of increase. Per cent.		Rate of increase. Per cent.
Ireland	2.45	Austria	1.30
Hungary	2.40	Bavaria	1.08
Spain	1.66	Netherlands	0.94
England	1.65	Naples	0.83
Rhenish Prussia	1.33	France	0.63

And more recently, Legoyt brings up these results to the close of 1846.[1] As shown by the census, the rate of increase was, in

	Per cent.		Per cent.
Great Britain, exclusive of Ireland	1.95	Sardinia	1.08
Prussia	1.84	Holland	0.90
Saxony	1.45	Austria	0.85
Norway	1.36	Sweden	0.83
		France	0.68

Or, as shown by the annual excess of births over deaths, and therefore more reliable: —

	Per cent.		Per cent.
Norway	1.30	Austria	0.90
Prussia	1.18	Saxony	0.90
Sweden	1.14	Hanover	0.85
Holland	1.03	Belgium	0.76
Wurtemberg	1.00	Bavaria	0.71
Great Britain, exclusive of Ireland	1.00	Russia	0.61
Denmark	0.95	France	0.50

In four departments of France, among which are two of the most thriving of Normandy, the deaths actually exceed the births.[2]

From the above facts, it would naturally be supposed that the percentage of births to the whole population must be smaller than in other European countries, and, from the lessened annual rate of increase of the population, that the proportionate number of births must be decreasing in similar ratio. This is found, indeed, to be the case.

[1] Journal des Economistes, May, 1847.

[2] Mill, Principles of Political Economy, i. p. 343.

From large statistics furnished by De Jonnés, we have compiled the following table of the comparative ratios of births to the population in the principal countries of Europe: —

	Ratio.		Ratio.
Venice and Dependencies, 1827	1 to 23	Sweden, 1825	1 to 28
Tuscany, 1834	,,	Holland, 1832	,,
Lombardy, 1828	1 to 24	Austria, 1829	,,
Russia, 1835	1 to 25	Belgium, 1836	,,
Wurtemberg, 1821 to 1827	,,	Bavaria, 1825	,,
Prussia, 1836	,,	Two Sicilies, 1831	,,
Mecklenburg, 1826	1 to 26	Sweden and Norway, 1828	1 to 30
Sardinia, 1820	,,	Denmark, 1833	,,
Naples and Dependencies, 1830	,,	Roman States, 1836	,,
Greece, 1828	,,	Turkey, 1835	,,
Poland, 1830	1 to 27	Hanover, 1835	1 to 31
Ireland, 1821 to 1831	,,	Sicily, 1832	,,
Germany, 1828	,,	Austria, 1828 to 1830	1 to 32
Switzerland, 1828	,,	Great Britain, 1821 to 1831	,,
Spain, 1826	,,	Scotland, 1821 to 1831	1 to 34
Portugal, 1815 to 1819	1 to 27.5	England, 1821 to 1831	1 to 35
		Norway, 1832	,,
		France, 1771 to 1851	1 to 25 to 1 to 37

In a total population, at different periods, of 232,673,000, there were 8,733,000 births; whence an average on the grand scale of one birth to every 26.6 individuals.

In France, however, the ratio has been steadily lessening, as seen by the following table: —

	Ratio of births.		Ratio of births.
1771 to 1775	1 to 25	1836 to 1840	1 to 34
1801 to 1810	1 to 30	1841 to 1845	1 to 35
1811 to 1825	1 to 32	1846 to 1850	1 to 37
1826 to 1836	1 to 33		

The position of France, as compared with the rest of Europe, in respect to the ratio of births to the population at different periods, is made still more manifest by another table: —

Annual ratio of births.	
1 to 23	Venetian Provinces, 1827; Tuscany, 1834.
1 to 23.5	Kingdom of Naples, 1822 to 1824.
1 to 24	Tuscany, 1818; Sicily, 1824; Lombardy, 1827 to 1828; Russia, 1831.
1 to 24.5	Prussia, 1825 to 1826.
1 to 25	France, 1781; Austria, 1827; Russia, 1835; Prussia, 1836.
1 to 26	Sardinia, 1820; Hanover, Wurtemberg, and Mecklenburg, 1826; Greece, 1828; Naples, 1830.
1 to 27	Spain, 1826; Germany and Switzerland, 1828; Poland, 1830; Ireland, 1831.
1 to 27.5	Portugal, 1815 to 1819.
1 to 28	Holland, 1813 to 1824; Bavaria and Sweden, 1825; Austria, 1829; Belgium, 1836.
1 to 29	Canton Lucerne, 1810; Holland, 1832.
1 to 29.8	France, 1801.
1 to 30	Sweden and Norway, 1828; Belgium, 1832; Denmark, 1833; Turkey, 1835; States of the Church, 1836.
1 to 31	Sicily, 1832; Hanover, 1835.
1 to 31.4	France, 1811.
1 to 31.6	France, 1821.
1 to 32	Austria, 1830; Great Britain and Switzerland, 1831.
1 to 33	France, 1828 to 1831.
1 to 34	Norway and Holstein, 1826; Scotland, 1831; France, 1834 to 1841.
1 to 35	Denmark, 1810; England, 1831; Norway, 1832.
1 to 37	France, 1851.

In Paris, strange to say, the decrease in the ratio of births to the population, though decided and steady, has not, in actual proportion, been as great as in the empire at large; showing that the cause, whatever we find it to be, is not one depending on the influence of a metropolis alone for its existence.

From 1817 to 1831, there averaged, in Paris, one birth to 26.87 inhabitants; but from 1846 to 1851, one to 31.98.[1]

2. Again, as might have been expected, we find that the proportion of still-births, in which we must include abortions, as has hitherto been done, however improperly, in all

[1] HUSSON, Les Consummations de Paris, 1856.

extensive statistics, is enormous, and is steadily increasing. To show this the more plainly, we first present a table of the ratio of still-births to the living births in the various countries of Europe.[1]

Geneva,[2] 1824 to 1833	1 to 17	Prague, 1820	1 to 30
Berlin Hospitals, 1758 to 1774	1 to 18	London Hospitals, 1749 to 1781	1 to 31
Paris Maternité,[3] 1816 to 1835	1 to 20	Vienna, 1823	1 to 32
Sweden, 1821 to 1825	1 to 23.5	Austria, 1828	1 to 49
Denmark, 1825 to 1834	1 to 24	France at large, 1853	1 to 24
Belgium,[4] 1841 to 1843	1 to 24.2	Department of Seine	1 to 15
Prussia,[5] 1820 to 1834	1 to 29	Paris,[6] 1836 to 1844	1 to 14.3
Iceland, 1817 to 1828	1 to 30	,, 1845 to 1853[7]	1 to 13.8

The proportion of still-births in the rural districts of France is governed by the same laws as in the metropolis.

In 363 provincial towns, the ratio was, from

1836 to 1845	1 to 19.55	1846 to 1850	1 to 18.8

While districts more thinly populated gave, from

1841 to 1845	1 to 29	1846 to 1850	1 to 27[8]

In Belgium, during a similar period, the ratio was much the same.[9]

1841 to 1843, in towns	1 to 16.1	1841 to 1843, in country	1 to 29.4

The apparent discrepancy between city and country, noticed as equally obtaining in Belgium and France, is chiefly owing to greater negligence of the country officials in registering the still-births, and to the fact, as we have seen

1 Compiled from De Jonnès.

2 10,925 births; 646 still-births.

3 Births, 52,538; still-births, 2,624.

4 Compiled from Quételet, Theory of Probabilities, p. 152. 406,073 living births; 16,767 still-births.

5 Births, 7,593,017; still-births, 257,068. 1839–41, 1 to 26.—Elliott, Hunt's Merchants' Magazine, July, 1856.

6 2,080 still-births.

7 2,349 still-births.

8 De Jonnès, loc. cit., p. 239.

9 Quételet, loc. cit., p. 152.

in Paris, that the ratio of births to the population is greater in the city than in the country at large.

Still again, while the proportion of still-births to the whole number is greatly increasing in Paris, so is the number of known abortions.

We omit, for the present, the evidence afforded by arrests and trials, which we might here have turned to account. At the Morgue, which represents but a very small fraction of the fœtal mortality of Paris, and in this matter almost only crime, there were deposited during the eighteen years preceding 1855, a total of 1,115 fœtuses,[1] of which 423 were at the full term, and 692 were of less than nine months; and of these last, 519, or five-sixths, were of not over six months, a large proportion of them showing decided marks of criminal abortion.

Again, of the 692 fœtuses of less than nine months deposited at the Morgue during these eighteen years, 295 were between 1836 to 1845, an average, at that time, of 32.7 yearly; and from 1846 to 1855 there were 397, an average of 44.1. During the means of these periods, the births in France were as follows:[2]—in 1841, 1,005,203; and, in 1851, 1,037,040; from which it is evident that there was deposited at the Morgue, in 1841, one infant, dead from abortion, to every 30,700 births; and, in 1851, one to every 23,500. The increased ratio is seen to be striking; it will hereafter become apparent that the increase is far greater in reality.

We turn now to our own country, to which the city of New York holds much the same relation, as respects public opinion no less than in other matters, that Paris holds to France.

Since 1805, when returns were first made to the Registry of New York, the number, proportionate as well as actual, of fœtal deaths, has steadily and rapidly increased. With a population at that time (1805) of 76,770, the number of

[1] Register of the Morgue. [2] De Jonnès, loc. cit., p. 193.

still and premature births was 47; in 1849, with a population estimated at 450,000, the number had swelled to 1,320.[1] Thus, while the population had increased only *six* times since 1805, the annual number of still and premature births had multiplied over *twenty-seven* times.

The following table shows the rapidity of this increase. The ratio of fœtal deaths to the population was in —

Year	Ratio	Year	Ratio
1805	1 to 1,633.40	1830	1 to 597.60
1810	1 to 1,025.24	1835	1 to 569.88
1815	1 to 986.46	1840	1 to 516.02
1820	1 to 654.52	1845	1 to 384.68
1825	1 to 680.68	1849	1 to 340.90

In the three years preceding 1849, there were registered in New York 400 premature births, and 3,139 children still-born, — a total of 3,539, representing at that time a yearly average of some 1,200 fœtal deaths. While it will be shown hereafter that a large proportion of the reported premature births must always be from criminal causes, and that though almost all the still-births at the full time, even from infanticide, are necessarily registered, but a small proportion of the abortions and miscarriages occurring are ever reported to the proper authorities, it will immediately be made apparent that, at the present moment, the abortion statistics of New York are far above those of 1849.

In the three years preceding 1857, there were registered in New York 1,196 premature, and 4,735 still births,[2] — a total of 5,931, representing a yearly average of some 2,000 fœtal deaths; showing that, in the short space of seven years, the number of fœtal deaths in New York, already enormous, had very nearly doubled.

Again, in 1856, the total number of births at the full time in New York was 17,755; of these, 16,199 were living;[3] proving that of children at the full time alone, setting aside

[1] Report of the City Inspector of New York for 1849.

[2] City Inspector's Report for 1856. [3] Ibid.

the great number of viable children born prematurely, and the innumerable earlier abortions not recorded, one in every 11.4 is born dead.

From foreign statistics on a large scale, it is found that the proportion of still-births, even allowing a wide margin for criminal causes, does not, in those countries, drop below 1 in 15, and this in France, ranging from that number up to 1 in 30 or 40 of the whole number of births reported. We have already given a table upon this point.[1]

In Geneva, out of 10,925 births occurring from 1824 to 1833, 1,221 of them being *illegitimate*, and therefore to be supposed liable to a large percentage of deaths from criminal causes, there were only 646 fœtal deaths; a proportion of 1 in 17.

In Belgium there were 29,574 *illegitimate* births from 1841 to 1843, and, of these, 1,766 were born still;[2] 1 in 16.8.

In New York, from 1854 to 1857, there were 48,323 births, and 5,931 still-births, at the full time and prematurely; or, in other words, 1 to every 8.1 was born dead.

The ratio of still-births in New York, including, as we have seen, abortions, is steadily increasing, as seen by the following table,[3] in which we have compared the still-births, supposable perhaps of accidental value, with the general mortality, whose value is at least as accidental, if not more so. The evidence, like that already furnished, is astounding.

1 Dr. E. M. Snow, of Providence, R. I., the very accurate Superintendent of Health of that city, writes us under date of 30th of January, 1868, that still-births in this country are as yet scarcely anywhere fully reported. "In Providence," he says, "I think we get nearly all of the still-born at full time, with a considerable number of the premature births. I report them all together, and report them under the head of still-born. The proportion of still-born to all the births in Providence from 1856 to 1866 inclusive, is 1 in 17.8."

2 Compiled from Quetelet, loc. cit., p. 152.

3 Compiled from City Inspector's Report for 1855.

	Total mortality.	Still-births.	Ratio.
1804 to 1809	13,128	349	1 to 37.6
1809 to 1815	14,011	533	1 to 26.3
1815 to 1825	34,798	1,818	1 to 19.1
1825 to 1835	59,347	3,744	1 to 15.8
1835 to 1855	289,786	21,702	1 to 13.3
1856 [1]	21,658	1,943	1 to 11.1
1868 [2]			1 to 10.5

The frequency of abortions and premature births reported from the practice of physicians, and thus to a certain extent, but not entirely, likely to be of natural or accidental origin, is as follows: —

In 41,699 cases registered by Collins, Beatty, La Chapelle, Churchill, and others,[3] there were 530 abortions and miscarriages. Here all the abortions were known: their proportion was 1 in 78.5.[4]

In New York, from 1854 to 1857, there were 48,323 births at the full time reported, and 1,196 premature. Here all the abortions were not known, probably but a very small fraction of them: the proportion was 1 in 40.4.

Finally, we compare the recorded premature still-births of New York with those still at the full time.

1 City Inspector's Report for 1856.

2 As stated by Dr. Elisha Harris, Registrar of Vital Statistics in New York, and member of the Metropolitan Board of Health (New-York Med. Gazette, 8 Feb. 1868, p. 155). This fact, and another given on a shortly ensuing page, go far to prove that our early deductions from the statistics of the city of New York cannot be wide from the truth. The effect of the attendance by uneducated midwives is insufficient to account for more than a fraction of the ratio existing, which is the rather to be explained by "the great frequency of applications for the production of abortion made to physicians by persons of high character and intelligence." (Prof. Elliot of New York, *Ibid.*)

3 Clay, Obstetric Cyclopædia, p. 21.

4 We have elsewhere shown that abortions from accidental causes, or from disease, are very much more frequent than is generally supposed (Boston Med. & Surg. Journal, Feb. 5, 1863). It must be recollected, however, that, so far from their relative number increasing from year to year, it must surely be decreasing. Our control of those maternal, fœtal, and placental diseases that may cause abortion, is steadily growing greater, and so is our ability to prevent the effect of most of the accidents that occur. The fact referred to tends, therefore, to strengthen rather than to weaken our argument.

In the seventeen years from 1838 to 1855,[1] there were reported 17,237 still-births at the full time, and 2,710 still prematurely; the last bearing the proportion of 1 to 6.3.

In the nine years, from 1838 to 1847, omitting 1842 for reasons stated below, there were 632 premature still-births, and 6,445 still at the full time; a yearly average of 1 in 10.2.

In the eight years, from 1848 to 1855, there were 2,078 premature still-births, and 10,792 still at the full time; an average of 1 in 5.

While in 1856 there were 387 still prematurely, and 1,556 at the full time; or 1 in 4.02.

From these figures there can be drawn but one conclusion, — that criminal abortion prevails to an enormous extent in New York, and that it is steadily and rapidly increasing. "We cannot refer," was well said by a former inspector of that city, "such a hecatomb of human offspring to natural causes."[2] We shall soon proceed to prove this point by other reasoning.

In 1868, much the same condition of things still obtains. Dr. Elisha Harris estimates that an eighth of all the still-births in New York are now at the seventh month, a time when the skill or ignorance of the accoucheur are of comparatively little importance with reference to the chance of so young a fœtus living. This proportion is of course greatly

[1] Separate records of the premature births in New York were not made before this period. They were not rendered in 1842; we have therefore omitted in the calculation the still-births of the same year. For a series of the official reports, we are indebted to the then City Inspector, Mr. George W. Morton.

It has been objected by a friend, with reference to the statistics of New York, that while for the past twenty-five years the returns of deaths, including still-births, have been very perfect, they were not so previously, and that, while the deaths and still-births are fully reported, the births never have been, and are not now, perhaps not even a fourth of them. If, however, to meet these points, we discard the earlier of the ratios given above, and examine only those that are calculated within the past twenty-five years, the irresistible conclusion remains the same.

[2] Inspector's Report of 1849.

increased by including the premature still-births occurring at all other periods of gestation.[1]

That our deductions concerning the population and births of France are perfectly legitimate, is admitted beforehand by the leading political economists of the day; ignorant as they were in its various relations of much of the evidence now brought forward, and of the conclusion to which the whole matter, directly and with almost mathematical exactness, is proved to tend.

"In France," remarks De Jonnés,[2] "the fecundity of the people is restrained within the strictest limits."

"The rate of increase of the French population," says Mill, "is the slowest in Europe;[3] the number of births not increasing at all, while the proportion of births to the population is considerably diminishing."[4]

We have seen, moreover, that in France the actual ratio of living births is constantly and rapidly diminishing, while the still-births, actual and proportional, are as fast increasing; that the premature births progress in similar ratio, and, by deduction and actual statistics, the criminal abortions; and that these facts obtain, not merely in the metropolis, but throughout the country.

What are the causes of these remarkable facts, need it now be asked? Let all allowances be made for certain conjugal habits extensively existing among the French, and by no means rarely imitated in this country; but the proportionate decrease of living births is too enormous, the actual and proportionate increase of premature and still births is too frightful to be wholly explained thus, or, as West,[5] Husson,[6] and De Jonnés[7] have thought, to be attributed to a mere progressive lack of fecundity. Reason,

[1] New-York Medical Gazette, 8 Feb. p. 155.
[2] Loc. cit., p. 195.
[3] Loc. cit., i. p. 344.
[4] Ibid., p. 343.
[5] Med. Times and Gazette, June, 1856, p. 611.
[6] Les Consummations de Paris.
[7] Loc. cit.

and the evidence alleged, compel us to believe that, in great measure, they are owing to criminal abortion.

Political economists allow the facts in France to be as we have stated. Their interpretation of the causes, unwilling as they would be to confess its ultimate bearing, we now compel to serve as evidence.

"They depend," according to one writer,[1] "either on physical agents, especially climate; or on the degree of civilization of a people, their domestic and social habits." — "In France, the climate is favorable to an increase of population; and this obstacle, this restraint, is found in its advanced civilization."[2]

"This diminution of births," says Legoyt,[3] "in the presence of a constant increase of the general population and of marriages, can be attributed to nothing else than wise and increased foresight on the part of the parent."

"The French peasant is no simple countryman, no downright 'Paysan du Danube;' both in fact and in fiction he is now 'le rusé paysan.' That is the stage which he has reached in the progressive development which *the constitution of things has imposed on human intelligence and human emancipation.*"[4]

"These facts are only to be accounted for in two ways. Either the whole number of births which nature admits of, and which happen in some circumstances, do not take place, or, if they do, a large proportion of those who are born, die. The retardation of increase results either from mortality or prudence; from Mr. Malthus's positive, or from his preventive check; and one or the other of these must and does exist, and very powerfully too, in all old societies. Wherever population is not kept down by the prudence of indi-

1 De Jonnés, loc. cit., p. 194.
2 Ibid., p. 195.
3 Journal des Economistes, 1847.
4 Mill, loc. cit., i. p. 336. The italics are our own. We shall hereafter refer back to this passage.

viduals or of the State, it is kept down by starvation or disease."[1]

But, on the other hand, it has been forgotten that the alternative supposed does not exist in the case we have instanced. Marriages in France, unlike some other Continental states, are continually increasing, and starvation and disease are yearly being shorn of their power. The authors quoted are therefore forced to a single position,—that the lessening of births can only be owing to "prudence" on the part of the community.

Moreover, it is allowed by Mill and by Malthus himself,[2] that so much of the decrease as cannot thus be explained, must be attributed to influences generally prevalent in Europe in earlier ages, and in Asia to the present time. "Throughout Europe these causes have much diminished, but they have nowhere ceased to exist."[3] Several of them have been named by the authority now quoted. Another, and greater than them all, he leaves unspoken: we are compelled to supply for him the omission.

The practice of destroying the fœtus *in utero*, to say nothing of infanticide, history declares to have obtained among all the earlier nations of the world, the Jews alone excepted, and to a very great extent. Aristotle defends it,[4] and Plato.[5] It is mentioned by Juvenal,[6] Ovid,[7] Seneca, and Cicero, and is denounced by the earlier Christians.[8] It was common in Europe through the middle ages, and still prevails among the Mohammedans,[9] Chinese,[10] Japanese,[11]

1 Ibid., i. p. 417.
2 Essay on Population.
3 Mill, loc. cit., i. p. 417.
4 Travels of Anacharsis, v. p. 270.
5 Ibid., iv. p. 342.
6 Satires, vi. v. 592.
7 Amor., lib. 2; Heroïdes, epist. 2.
8 Reeve's Apologies.
9 Blaquiere, Letters from the Med., pp. 90, 184; Slade, Records of Travels, ii. p. 162.
10 Barrow, Travels in China, p. 113; De Pauw, Philosoph. Dissert.; Medhurst, China, &c., p. 45; Smith, Exploratory Visit, &c., i. p. 53.
11 Golownin, Memoirs of a Captivity, iii. p. 222.

Hindoos,[1] and most of the nations of Africa and Polynesia,[2] to such an extent, that we may well doubt whether more have ever perished in those countries by plague, by famine, and the sword.

[1] MOOR, Hindoo Infanticide, p. 63; BUCHANAN, Christian Researches in Asia, p. 49; WARD, View of the History, &c., of the Hindoos, p. 393.

[2] For a long list of authorities on these points, see BECK, Med. Jurisprudence, ii. p. 389 et seq.

Through the kindness of a friend, Dr. D. F. LINCOLN, our attention has been called to a late paper by Dr. STRICKER, of Frankfort-on-the-Main, who considers that the relative frequency of the crime in Christian as compared with other nations has not yet been sufficiently appreciated, either by ethnographers or physicians, owing to the fact, that, while in heathen countries the practice is resorted to with an openness which courts observation, in Europe its evidences are confined, in great measure, to the annals of criminal administration, and are therefore comparatively unknown. This writer furnishes us with much interesting evidence of the frequency of abortion in uncivilized countries, which does not seem as yet to have been presented to the English reader, a portion of which I will here give. "LORENZ RIGLER, whilom teacher of clinical medicine in Constantinople (Die Türkei und deren Bewohner; Wien 1850), says that along with the causes of the premature old age of the Turkish women, their usually irregular menstruation, their hemorrhages and numerous other diseases of the sexual organs, and their infecundity, must be reckoned the measures which they take to expel the fruit of their bodies, with the intention of preventing a numerous family, for financial reasons, or to preserve their beauty. Pregnancy in the unmarried is always interrupted by violence, Jewesses being commonly employed. The Government treats those detected in giving drugs for this purpose with great severity.

"Similar accounts are given by the former body physician to the Shah of Persia, and teacher in the medical school at Teheran, Dr. Jacob Edward Polak (Persien, das Land und seine Bewohner; Leipzig, 1863, 1, p. 216), who, after a nine years' residence in that country, states that all pregnancies outside of marriage end with abortion, the membranes being ruptured with a hook. This operation is executed by midwives of whom there were several in Teheran, well known and much sought after on this account. The business is carried on quite openly, and no hindrance is opposed. Only a few unhappy creatures try to assist themselves; these apply quantities of leeches, are bled in the feet, take emetics of sulphate of copper, drastic purgatives, or the sprouts of date-stones, and, if all these means fail, they cause their abdomen to be beaten, and walked over; many perishing under the effects of this rough treatment. But nowhere in Persia does the evil custom prevail, which is universal among the higher classes of Turkey, that the woman, after bearing two children, for the future provokes abortion, with the knowledge of her husband, partly to preserve her form and beauty, and partly to diminish the number of her descendants. MACMURDO found in Cutch, the peninsula north of Bombay, that abortion is an universal custom. — RITTER, Erdkunde, vi. p. 1054."

It is evident, therefore, that the actual and proportionate increase of still-births, — and, by induction, setting aside all probable cases of infanticide, of abortion, — and the comparative increase of a population, reciprocally influence and govern each other so completely, that from the one it may in any given case be almost foreseen what the other must prove.

It is impossible that the results quoted from the registry of New York, any more than those of France, even if so far, can in any great measure be owing to natural causes alone. They are wholly inexplicable on any principles "which do not recognize an amount of guilt at which humanity shudders." In comparing that city with Paris, certain allowances must indeed be made: abroad, for the effects of wars and conscription, of despotism, and of migration outward; at home, for the effects of governmental laxity, and of migration inward. In both cities, the amount of prostitution, an element not to be lost sight of, must be nearly the same; and in both, under the constant progress of science, medical and hygienic, the ratio of fœtal mortality, unless induced by criminal causes, may year by year be supposed to have been steadily diminished.

We have seen, that in New York, in the absence of all influences that tend to keep down population in foreign countries, old and crowded, and under the yoke of despotism, the effects, attributable elsewhere to these causes, exist, and to a greater degree than in any other country:

That the ratio of fœtal deaths to the population had swelled from 1 in 1633, in 1805, to 1 in 340, in 1849; while in France at a later period, 1851, they were only about 1 in 1000:

That the actual number of fœtal deaths in seven years, from 1850 to 1857, had very nearly doubled:

That the fœtal deaths, as compared with the total of births, — elsewhere in cases of illegitimacy, where the results are the very worst, and where crime is confessed to have produced them, being 1 in 16.8,[1]—had here, legitimate and natural, reached the frightful ratio of 1 in 8.1:

That the fœtal deaths, as compared with the total mortality, had increased from 1 in 37, in 1805, to 1 in 13, in 1855; and to 1 in 10.5, in 1868:

That the reported early abortions, of which the greater number of course escape registry, bear the ratio to the living births of 1 in 4.04, while elsewhere they are only 1 in 78.5:

And, finally, that early abortions, bearing the proportion to the still-births at the full time of 1 in 10.2, in 1846, had increased to 1 in 4.02, in 1856.

It must be borne in mind, that these statistics are positive, proving the existence of a certain number of pregnancies abruptly terminated. They cannot, therefore, be controverted by any argument regarding means for the prevention of pregnancy, no matter to what extent these may be used. Nor should it be forgotten, that, for every registered premature birth or abortion, innumerable ones occur that are never recorded.

Almost doubling, therefore, as does New York, the worst of those fearful ratios of fœtal mortality existing in Europe, it is not strange that our metropolis has been held up, even by a Parisian, to the execration of the world. "On le voit (l'avortement)," says Tardieu, "en Amérique, dans une grande cité comme New York, constituer une industrie véritable et non poursuivie."

In this description of New York, we have that of the country.[2] The relative annual increase of the population

[1] Belgium.

[2] Local exceptions to this general rule will of course be found to exist, as is always the case with laws based on mere statistics, especially, as here, where reports to the registry are liable, for evident reasons, to be withheld. Thus it appears from Dr. Jewell's collections (North American Medico-Chirurgical Review, March, 1857, p. 277), that the proportion of still-births in Philadelphia was, in 1856, only 1 in 913 to the total population, and 1 in 20.1 to the general mortality, against which evidence must be placed that which we subsequently furnish from Professor Hodge.

existing throughout America, depending as this does chiefly on immigration, must not mislead us. The ratio of fœtal death in the metropolis surpasses what has ever been dreamed to obtain even in old countries, where innumerable more legitimate causes for it might be thought to exist. At Boston, which for morals is allowed to compare favorably with any city of its size in the Union, "undoubtedly more than a hundred still-births yearly escape being recorded, a large proportion of which, no doubt, result from criminal abortion."[1] And our public prints, far and wide, even in the smaller towns and villages, constantly chronicle deaths from the commission of the crime.[2]

It will be seen that the tables we have now given, and the calculations from which they are deduced, are mainly brought down to no later period than the year 1860. At the present date (1868), our time is so completely occupied by the

[1] MS. Letter from City Registrar, March 26, 1857. In a late number of the Philadelphia Medical and Surgical Reporter, it is stated that the efficient Registrar of the city of Boston, Mr. Apollonio, has seen reason to retract the above opinion. This, however, is not the case. He has just written us (1868) as follows : "I have not changed my opinion, and am at a loss to account for the statement. I think I am right in inferring what is obvious to every one who reflects at all on the matter: 1. That there are fewer marriages than there should be; 2. That fewer births result from these marriages than ought to proceed therefrom; 3. That the cause of the above facts is not a *good* or *satisfactory* one, in *any* point of view."

[2] Shortly after the above was first written, the report of the committee appointed in 1858 to investigate the Health Department of the city of New York appeared; and we found that our statements regarding the frequency of the crime in the metropolis were fully corroborated. Not merely were additional official statistics on this point given (pp. 182, 183), but valuable testimony from Drs. GRISCOM (pp. 25, 30), MCNULTY (p. 55), FRANCIS (p. 64), and BULKLEY (p. 133). Dr. REESE's paper on Infant Mortality, republished by the committee (pp. 90–100) from the Transactions of the American Medical Association for 1857, also contains incidental reference to the frequency of abortion, and, for its direct and earnest dealing with the subject, deserves unqualified commendation. Valuable evidence is also given by Dr. SANGER, of New York, in his work upon Prostitution.

In this connection, we would call attention to the evidence of the extent of the crime in Boston, afforded since our own remarks upon that point were first in type, by Professor WALTER CHANNING. (Boston Med. and Surg. Journal, March 17, 1859.)

duties of an engrossing practice, that it is impossible for us even to present the mass of statistical material that has since accrued, much less to institute careful comparisons between the different series of years. To do so is, however, now unnecessary; for, while we have no doubt that our conclusions would all be borne out by the added results of later years, they have received such proof from the direct evidence that has since been afforded by medical practitioners, as to render any further labor of the kind we have hitherto presented, simply a work of supererogation. As a single instance, however, of the completeness with which the more thorough investigations of the present day tend to corroborate our conclusions, we will present the statistics of one of our smaller towns, Amherst, Mass., tabulated to within the past year. They were compiled, and furnished us, by our friend, Professor Edward Hitchcock, of that place, in March, 1867.

"On account of some statements made by a correspondent upon the subject of 'Vital Statistics,' — such as that the births and deaths for 21 years could be the only fair basis for a calculation, — our very accurate and courteous town clerk, Mr. Carter, has furnished a complete table of all the births and deaths in town for the past 21 years, and the number of deaths under one year (including still-born), and those under 21 years.

	Births.	Deaths.	Deaths under 1 year.	Deaths under 21 years.
1846	72	56	16	33
1847	72	26	4	9
1848	83	67	7	39
1849	68	70	11	34
1850	74	66	17	37
1851	80	75	11	42
1852	77	43	9	19
1853	79	49	6	20
1854	59	60	8	23
1855	61	42	6	16
1856	67	40	2	8
1857	68	54	12	30

	Births.	Deaths.	Deaths under 1 year.	Deaths under 21 years.
1858	61	60	11	32
1859	50	57	12	29
1860	73	57	16	27
1861	80	57	7	30
1862	69	55	7	23
1863	67	49	5	13
1864	65	85	7	28
1865	74	63	10	24
1866	95	42	5	15

Total births for 21 years, 1,494.
Total deaths for 21 years, 1,173.
Deaths under 1 year, 189.
Deaths under 21 years, 531.
Average annual births for 21 years, 71.
Average annual deaths for 21 years, 56.
Proportion of births to deaths for 21 years, 9 to 7 (nearly), 1 to 0.785.
Proportion of births to deaths from 1846 to 1855, 1 to 0.764.
Proportion of births to deaths from 1856 to 1866, 1 to 0.804.
Calculated proportion of births to deaths for 21 years, 1 to 0.400.

"Suppose that we divide these 21 years into two periods, one from 1846 to 1855 inclusive, and from 1856 to 1866 inclusive, and see what has been the death-rate for these periods. In the first one, it has been at the rate of 764 deaths for every 1,000 births; and, in the last one, at the rate of 804 to every 1,000, or an increase of 4 per cent. It ought to be mentioned, however, that, in the count of deaths for 1864, there were 19 reckoned as deaths in Amherst, which really did not take place in town, but were citizens of Amherst serving in the Union army, and either were killed in battle or died in hospital. This, however, would reduce the average but slightly, making the rate to be 780 to every 1,000, instead of 804 to 1,000. Taking, then, the lowest actual death-rate, we find that the difference between the first and second period is sixteen-thousandths; or the fact is, that, out of every 1,000 deaths, there were 16 more in the second than in the first period.

"Let us now try to arrive at the same conclusions in

another way, by comparing the births of the five-years period from 1846 to 1850 inclusive, with consecutive five-year periods. In this comparison, we find that the births from 1846 to 1850 are to —

The deaths from 1851 to 1855 as 1 to 0.749.
The same from 1856 to 1860 as 1 to 0.746.
The same from 1862 to 1866 as 1 to 0.805.

Or still in another way, —

Deaths from 1846 to 1850, 285.
Deaths from 1861 to 1865, 309.
Births from 1846 to 1850, 379.
Births from 1861 to 1865, 355.

"By which we see that in the first period the deaths were less, and the births greater, than in the latter period, when the population of the town exceeded the former period by probably 700 persons.

"Or, more exactly, the births from 1842 to 1851 were 753, and those from 1857 to 1867 were 702; also the deaths from 1842 to 1851 were 577, and those from 1857 to 1867 were 579. So that in the last decade we have 51 less births than we had in the first, and 2 more deaths, and that in spite of an increased population from immigration.

"In a condensed form, then, this fact is presented to us, that the town of Amherst 20 years ago, with a population numbering about 2,550, had annually a greater number of births than it now has, with a population of about 3,200; and that the deaths of the town in the above-mentioned periods are almost exactly the same.

"Let us adduce another phase under this branch of vital statistics.

"The number of births in Amherst from 1842 to 1866 inclusive is 1,799. The number of intentions of marriage, as registered by the town clerk during the same period, is 772. This gives an annual average for these 25 years of a little more than two children for each of these published intentions (2.343). If now we take the same proportion for the years of 1842 to 1846; we find the result to be nearly three children (2.892); and, if we make the same proportion on the five-year period from 1862 to 1866, the result is a little more than one child (1.156), or a difference of nearly two children (1.736).

"If, however, any one should think that similar estimates from the *actual* marriages would be more valuable than from the intentions of marriage, it may be said that from 1842 to 1846 the proportion is 3.377, and from 1862 to 1866 is 2.334, or a difference of about one child. The record of intentions of marriage, however, may be regarded as more surely indicating the number of marriages than the record of marriages actually solemnized in the town."

In one of his late reports to the Legislature of Massachusetts, the efficient and thoughtful Secretary of the Board of State Charities, Mr. F. B. Sanborn, thus comments upon the fact now alluded to, — the decrease of the excess of our births over the deaths: —

"It may be interesting to notice here some observations made, and statistics given, by Dr. William Farr, of London, in a paper read before the Social Science Congress at Manchester early in October, 1866. Dr. Farr's paper shows, so far as public health is concerned, that England ranks next to Sweden and Norway, which are the most highly favored countries of Europe in this respect, the death-rate in them being so low as 17 annually in the 1,000 of population. In Great Britain and Ireland it averages 22, and in France it is also 22; so that the two countries seem to be on a par. But while the annual increase of population in Great Britain, (due chiefly to the excess of births over deaths) is upwards of 14,000 per million of the population, in France it is scarcely more than 4,000. The annual rate of increase in France is less than half that of Holland, only as 4 to 11 compared with Denmark, and as 4 to 13 to Prussia. That these figures of Dr. Farr are mainly correct, we have no reason to doubt; but it seems that the excess of births over deaths in the city of Paris (with a population of about 1,725,000) is considerably greater than the above-named rate of 4,000 to the million. The statistics of Paris for the second quarter of 1866 prove that, from the 1st of April to the 1st of July, 13,405 children were born, being 263 males in excess of females. 9,601 of these children were legitimate, and 3,854 illegitimate. Among these latter, 960 were not recognized. During the same period, 4,877 marriages were contracted. 11,114 deaths occurred, of which 5,780 were males. The average number of deaths in Paris was 122 per day. Admitting that this excess of births over deaths is a fair average for the year, we have the annual excess of 9,164, or at the rate of about 5,300 to every million of the population. The rate in Massachusetts for the eight years 1856–1863 was less than 10,000 to the million, but yet nearly double that of Paris.

"How comes it, we may inquire, that with conditions of public health equal to what exist in England, and far superior (as Dr. Farr's figures show) to those of Germany, the French people should have become almost stationary in numbers? This surely is a curious and interesting question to study; for it goes to the very root of national stability, and becomes an important one to us, when we reflect that our own State is approximating to this condition of France,—the excess of births over deaths being yearly diminished, except as affected by the great disturbing forces of war and peace. In France it has been suggested that the abstraction of 400,000 young men from the flower of the population to supply the army affords a partial explanation; the large numbers of persons under religious vows of celibacy has also been assigned; besides what is styled the *social evil*. But this is not peculiar to France. We might be inclined partly to account for the fact by the scandalous neglect to which infants are abandoned in Paris and the great towns; but the statistics of mortality seem to forbid this. At any rate, there exists a very large amount of infant mortality in France, far exceeding that of Massachusetts, painful as our own statistics are. On this subject there is a great deal more to be said, for which I have now neither the time nor the necessary statistics, concerning the prevention and the destruction of offspring, and the other matters related to it."[1]

In the State of Massachusetts at large, it has been found of late years that "the increase of the population, or the excess of the births over the deaths, has been *wholly* of those of *recent foreign origin;*"[2] this in 1850. In 1853 "it is evident that the births within the Commonwealth, with the usual increase, have resulted in favor of foreign parents in an increased ratio."[3] In other words, it is found that in so far as depends upon the American and native element, and in the absence of the existing immigration from abroad, the population of Massachusetts is stationary or decreasing.[4]

For several years since the preceding paragraphs were

1 Third Report of the Mass. Board of State Charities, 1866, p. 31.

2 CHICKERING, Comparative View of the Population of Boston, 1850; City Document, No. 60, p. 44.

3 Twelfth Registration Report to the Legislature of Massachusetts, 1853, p. 116. The truth of this statement has been corroborated by Dr. CURTIS, in his Report on the Census of Boston in 1855. City Document, 1856, p. 22. Also, Fifteenth State Registration Report, 1856, p. 179.

4 "Had the rate of the annual increase of the numbers living under the age of five (3.13 per cent) resulted entirely from the increase of births in a permanent population, the number of births of 1855 (in the districts where the ratio of the registered deaths to the population was greater than one to sixty-three, 166 of the 331 towns (would have been 24,457, instead of 23,481,) the number registered. On the other hand, had the increase resulted wholly from migration (the annual number of births in the permanent population being constant), the number of births would have been only 22,956. The number of births registered is somewhat nearer the latter than the former of these two values.

"Assuming the correctness of the births, deaths, and population, in the selected districts, it appears that 35 per cent of the increase of the population under the age of five was due to births in the permanent portion of the population, and 65 per cent due to the movement of the migratory portion; also, that 38 per cent of the increase of population at all ages was due to excess of births over deaths, leaving 62 per cent to be accounted for by excess of immigration over emigration." — ELLIOTT, The Laws of Human Mortality in Massachusetts; Proceedings of Am. Assoc. for Adv. of Science, Montreal, 1857, p. 57.

written, this question of the dying-out of the native population has been carefully investigated by statisticians, more especially Drs. Snow, of Providence, R. I., to whose labors I have already referred, and Nathan Allen, of Lowell, Mass., a member of the Board of State Charities. Dr. Allen has been indefatigable in calling the attention of investigators to this important question, through the media of legislative reports, the medical, and the public press. His results seem identical with those I had myself presented, as will be seen by the following summary of them, published by Dr. Allen in 1866: —

"From 1850 to 1866, the fifteen registration reports of Massachusetts return 208,730 births of strictly foreign parentage, besides 22,376 not stated, a large portion of which must be foreign. All of these living when the census is taken, would be considered, according to present usage, American; whereas they should be counted strictly under the foreign head. A careful analysis of the census and registration reports presents the following facts: —

"The increase of population in the State has been confined principally to cities and towns where manufacturing, mechanical, and commercial business is carried on. In the purely agricultural districts, there has been very little increase of population. Railroads have had a powerful influence in changing the population of the State from the hills and country towns to the valleys and plains. Wherever water-power or steam-power has been introduced, or where trade and commerce has found advantages, there population has greatly increased. The eastern section of the State has increased far more than the middle or western districts. Population in manufacturing places has increased about five times more than in agricultural districts. It is found, also, wherever there has been much or a rapid increase of population, it has been made up largely of a foreign element. Now, if a line could be drawn exactly between the American and foreign population as it respects this increase, it would throw much light upon the subject. According to the census of 1860, it appears that two counties — Dukes and Nantucket — had actually decreased in population. There were eighty-six towns also which had diminished in population between 1850 and 1860. In a small part of these towns, this change is accounted for by the fact that some section of the place had, in the mean time, been set off to another town. The places in the State that have increased the least, or declined in population, are found to be settled generally with American stock.

"A serious question here arises, Is there a *natural* increase in this class of the community? It is generally admitted, that foreigners have a far greater number of children, for the same number of inhabitants, than the Americans. It is estimated by some physicians, that the same number of married persons of the former have, on an average, three times as many children as an equal number of those of the latter. This gives the foreign element great power of increase of population, — derived not so much from emigration as from the births exceeding greatly the deaths. It is alleged that great numbers of Americans move out of the State, and that this accounts for their apparent decrease in population. It should be remembered, also, that large numbers of the same class move every year into this State from other States. If we take, from the census of 1860, the difference between the number of persons from Massachusetts living in other States, and those born in other States residing in this State, the gain in this difference, from 1850 to 1860, was less than 11,000. It is evident from this fact, that the actual loss of population of purely American origin by emigration is not very great, amounting to less than three thousand persons annually. In this three thousand persons, allowance is made for filling the places of those deceased natives of Massachusetts residing in other States, in excess of the number of persons deceased in this State, but natives of other States. This general statement deserves repetition;

that is, that the strictly-American population of Massachusetts is not diminished by emigration annually three thousand persons over and above the number of the same class moving from other States into this State. But the question of *natural* increase is far more important; for, if the increase from this source is small or none at all, the loss of three thousand persons every year from the best portion of our population becomes a very serious matter.

"It has been alleged that the births are not all reported. For many years after the registration laws went into force, it is well known that this was the fact; but of late years there are reasons to believe that pretty full returns are made. The United States census for 1860 reports under one year of age in Massachusetts 31,312 persons. The Registration Report of the State returns for the same year 36,051 births, and 4,821 deaths of infants under one year of age, which leaves living 31,230, only eighty-two less than the census. These separate results are obtained by two distinct agencies, and modes of collecting the statistics entirely different, so that there could be no collusion or repetition. We have not the same means to verify in other years. The Registration Report for 1864 gives 30,449 births and 28,723 deaths; for 1865, 30,249 births and 26,152 deaths; making only 1,726 births in 1864 more than the deaths, and 4,097 more in 1865. Now, since the foreign population have two or three times as many children as the same number of married persons among the Americans, — a fact well established, — is it not very evident that the strictly American deaths exceed the births? In examining the reports, it appears that the counties containing the least foreign population return in 1864 and 1865 more deaths than births. Take the towns containing none or scarce any foreign population, where in 1864 and 1865 not a single birth is reported (there are thirty-four such towns in the State), and the whole number of deaths in these towns for 1864 and 1865 exceeds each year the births. On the other hand, an examination of those cities and towns containing a large foreign element shows that the whole number of births there invariably exceeds the deaths.

"There is a difficulty in discriminating in the registration reports between the deaths of Americans and of foreigners, since the deaths of all those of foreign origin born in this country are understood to be returned as Americans. This mode of reporting the deaths is unfortunate where it is desirable to ascertain the *natural* increase of population in the two classes separately. Still, very correct knowledge upon this subject can be obtained in any city by a careful examination of the books of the undertakers, the superintendent of burials, and of the city clerk, together with the places of burial. In the cities of Lowell and Lawrence, where there is a very large foreign element, we have obtained from these sources the exact number of deaths, foreign and American, for 1864 and 1865; and the number of deaths in the former city over the births were rising one hundred each year, and in Lawrence, for the two years, they were over one hundred.

"In a report upon the comparative view of the population of Boston in 1849 and 1850, made to the city government November, 1851, Dr. Jesse Chickering, after a most careful analysis of the births and deaths in Boston, states that 'the most important fact derived from this view, is the result that the whole increase of population, arising from the excess of births over deaths for these two years, has been among the foreign population.' Since 1850, we think it will be very difficult to prove that there has been any *natural* increase of population in Boston with the strictly American population.

"It may be said the force of the statistics from the Registration Reports of 1864 and 1865 is very much impaired by the effects of the war. The births may have been somewhat diminished, and the deaths increased, by such means; but then the foreign element would have been affected as well as the American, since it was largely represented in the war. But a similar state of things in reference to the increase of the two classes existed for years before the war; and there is abundant evidence to prove that for a long time there has been a relative decrease of births with the Americans. In the colonial census of 1765, taken one hundred years ago, when the main population was purely American, the total inhabitants were then 222,563, and the number under sixteen years of age returned as 102,489,—almost one-half of the whole population. Now it is estimated, that only about one-third of our population is under fifteen years of age. According to this estimate, a careful analysis of the natural proportion of the children to each class will show that scarcely one-fifth of the Americans are at the present time under sixteen years of age. This makes a surprising difference in the relative number of children of the same people at the two periods, 1765 and 1865.

"Again, many towns in the State have been settled over two hundred years, and their history will include from six to eight generations. The records of several of these towns have been carefully examined with respect to the relative number of children in each generation. It was found, that the families comprising the first generation, had, on an average, between eight and ten children; the next three generations averaged between seven and eight to each family; the fifth generation about five, and the sixth less than three, to each family. What a change as to the size of the families since those olden times! Then, large families were common; now, the exception. Then, it was rare to find married persons having only one, two, or three children: now, it is very common. Then, it was regarded a calamity for a married couple to have no children: now, such calamities are found on every side of us; in fact, they are fashionable.

"It is the uniform testimony of physicians who have been extensively engaged in the practice of medicine twenty, thirty, forty, and fifty years in this State,—and who have the best possible means of understanding this whole subject, — that there has been gradually a very great falling-off in the number of children among American families.

"Two general remarks should here be made: 1st, That this decrease of children is found to prevail in country towns and rural districts almost to the same extent as in the cities, which is contrary to the general impression; 2d, From the bills of mortality, it is an established fact, that, on an average, only about three-fifths of all persons born, including the city and the country, ever live to reach adult life. It will be seen at once, that with this rate of mortality, if the deaths exceed every year the births, or are only slightly in excess, the children will not keep the original stock good in point of numbers. In view of these facts, several questions naturally arise. If the foreign population in Massachusetts continues to increase as it has, and the American portion remains stationary, or decreases, as the probabilities indicate, what will be the state of society here twenty-five, fifty, or a hundred years hence? How long will it be before the foreign portion will outnumber the American in our principal cities and towns, or constitute even a majority in the whole Commonwealth?

"The cause why there should be such a difference in the number of children, between the American families now upon the stage, and those of the same stock one, two, and three generations ago, is a subject of grave inquiry. Again, why should there be such a difference in this respect between American families, and those of the English, German, Scotch, and Irish of the present day? Is this difference owing to our higher civilization, or to a more artificial mode of life and the unwholesome state of society? Or can it be attributed to a degeneracy in the physical condition and organization of females, or a settled determination with the married to have no children, or a very limited number?"[1]

[1] Third Annual Report of the Secretary of the Board of State Charities of Mass., 1866, p. 27. The above paper has given rise to much discussion. A

"This result will doubtless surprise many, who will hardly think it possible. Is it general, or is it accidental? If it be general, how has it happened? What causes have been in operation to produce it? How is it to be accounted for?"[1] These questions have hitherto been unanswered. We shall find, however, their solution only too easy.

writer in the Philadelphia Medical and Surgical Reporter of 24 Nov. 1866, asserts that a clearer distinction should have been recognized between nativity and parentage, and that, if this had been done, the bearing of the statistics would have been materially changed. Dr. SNOW, moreover, in a subsequent number of the Reporter (Jan. 1867), has taken a similar view, and writes us concerning the deficiencies of the Massachusetts registration reports in the respect referred to, saying that, however true the fact may be of those towns where Americans and foreigners are more nearly balanced, it cannot be so over the whole State. We have, however, been unable to perceive the force of these objections, inasmuch as the statistics originally presented seem reliable so far as they have been collected. Waiving, however, this point, Dr. SNOW admits the whole question, when he allows that, though there may have "always been, in a series of years, an actual gain (of the American population), as compared with the foreign there is probably a relative loss." Had Dr. CHICKERING in the paper written in 1850, from which we have quoted, stated that the excess of births over the deaths was *chiefly*, instead of *wholly*, of those of recent foreign origin, there could have been no possible exception taken to the truth of the statement. We may say, moreover, in this connection, that our friend, Dr. SNOW, who is still engaged in investigating this subject, and in whose fairness and desire to arrive at an impartial conclusion we have great confidence, writes us under date of 4 Feb. 1868, subsequently to the letter we have quoted, that, while he believes much of the apparent decrease in our American population is owing to the systematic prevention of pregnancy, — a point to which we have already referred, — and to other causes rather than to abortion, yet that he is much nearer our position than when he began to investigate. "I am satisfied," he says, "that the crime of abortion is much more frequent and wide-spread than I had supposed, and that there is need of every effort to suppress it;" and he shows us, in his Registration Report of the City of Providence for the month of February, 1868, as an interesting fact, that, while there was an *increase* of 103 marriages in 1866, there was a *decrease* of 8 births in 1867. The Boston Daily Advertiser of 17 Jan. 1867, presents the question very fairly in an editorial which has not merely attracted attention at home, but excited much abroad. Had we space, we should quote from M. CARLIER, of Paris, known in this country by his work, Le Mariage aux Etats Unis. In a letter seeking information concerning the acclimation of races in the United States, and communicated to us by his translator, Dr. B. J. JEFFRIES, this author lays much stress upon the value of the article referred to.

[1] CHICKERING, loc. cit., p. 49.

Amid such general thrift and wealth, there has been every reason for the native, like the foreign population, to increase. The preventive check of the economists, though undoubtedly present, can have played but an inferior part, as we shall prove. Emigration westward, the only apparent positive check, though extensive, cannot wholly account for the result.

But statistics exist by whose light we may read this important problem.[1]

In 1850, the ratio of births to the population of Massachusetts, foreign and American combined, was 1 in 36,[2] and in 1855, 1 in 34;[3] a ratio much smaller than that obtaining in most countries of Europe, and about equalling that of France, which, in 1850, was 1 in 37.

In 1855, the ratio of still-births, at the full time and premature, as compared with the living births, was 1 to 15.5.[4] In France it is 1 to 24; in Austria, 1 to 49.

In 1851, the ratio of fœtal deaths to the general mortality was 1 to 13.3;[5] in 1855, 1 to 10.4.[6] In New-York City, in 1856, it was 1 to 11. In any city we should expect to find the proportion much greater than in a State at large; we here find it less.

The ratio of premature births to those at the full time, during the period from 1850 to 1856, was 1 to 26.1.[7] In

1 The tables now presented, we prepared in 1857, from the fifteen Registration Reports of the State of Massachusetts then published. Advance sheets of the Sixteenth Report were kindly furnished us while our first article was passing through the press, by the compiler, Dr. JOSIAH CURTIS, of Boston. The premature births for 1856 and 1857 were not given in the reports for those years, so that we could not extend our calculations beyond 1855. Deductions from the still-births at the full time, which were alone given in the years referred to, are of course useless for the present inquiry.

2 Births, 27,664; population, 994,665.

3 Births, 32,845; population, 1,132,369.

4 Total births at full time, 32,845; living births at full time, 32,120; fœtal deaths, 2,064; still, at full time, 725; premature, 1,339.

5 Total deaths, including 1,462 fœtal, 19,461.

6 Total deaths, including 2,064 fœtal, 21,523.

7 Births at full time, 154,245; premature, 5,899.

New York, in 1857, it was 1 to 40, and in good medical practice it is found, as we have seen, to be 1 in 78.[1]

In comparing the recorded abortions and premature births in the city of New York with the still-births there occurring at the full time, we found that the former had varied from 1 in 10, in 1838, to 1 in 4, in 1856.

In the State of Massachusetts it appears that, during the fourteen years and eight months preceding 1855, there were recorded 4,570 still-births, and 11,716 premature births and abortions,[2] the ratio being 1 abortion to .3 still-birth; or, in other words, it would appear from the statistics quoted, that the comparative frequency of abortions in Massachusetts is thirteen times as great as in the worst statistics of the city of New York. We are willing however, we rejoice, to modify this statement,—as, in the earliest of the years quoted, returns from the city of Boston seem to have been imperfect or wanting,—and to confine our calculations to a more recent period.

From 1850 to 1855, the registration being much more accurate than before, and its results compiled with the greatest care, three years of the five, by a noted statistician, Dr. Shurtleff, there were recorded in Massachusetts 2,976 still-births, and 5,899 premature births and abortions,[3] the ratio being 1 abortion to .5 still-birth; in other words, the frequency of abortions, as compared with still-births at the full time, seems at least eight times as great in Massachusetts as in the worst statistics of the city of New York.

In the above remarks, we must not be misunderstood. We believe Massachusetts no worse with regard to abortion than many other portions of the country, but that its registration, however imperfect, is conducted with greater care. From the statistics given, it may easily be surmised what the amount of this crime *must be elsewhere*. It is necessarily of

[1] We have hitherto shown that the argument from this fact can be very materially strengthened.

[2] Fourteenth Registration Report, 1855.

[3] Ibid.

infinitely more common occurrence than infanticide, the murder of children after birth, for proof of the frequency of which, at the present moment, in Great Britain, we refer to Dr. Burke Ryan's Fothergillian Essay[1] on the subject, and to the current medical periodicals.

It must not be forgotten, that, while nearly every still-birth at the full time is necessarily recorded, there must be but very few registrations of the premature births and abortions actually occurring; that, though the contrary seems here the case, such occurrences are generally, as they would be supposed, far more frequent in crowded cities than in country districts, or in a State at large; and that, however great may be the influence of the prevention of pregnancy in repressing a population, these constitute proofs of pregnancies actually occurring, and frequently criminally terminated.

Few persons could have believed possible the existence of such frightful statistics, the result toward which they must be confessed inevitably to tend, or the dread cause from which they spring. Either these statistics must be thrown aside as utterly erroneous and worthless, or they must be accepted with their conclusions. We would gladly do the former; but they present too many constant quantities, in other respects,[2] for this to be allowed. Our own calculations were made with care, and we have presented the elements on which they rest. In asserting the results, at once so awful and astounding, we desire to fix upon them the attention and scrutiny of the world.

We have seen that the increase of the population of Massachusetts by living births is almost exclusively among its

[1] London Sanitary Review, July, 1859. See also the London Lancet of corresponding date, &c.

[2] As, for instance, in the regularly progressive series of deaths and births as compared with the population; constant also as compared with each other. Population of Massachusetts: by census of 1850, 994,665; 1855, 1,132,369. Deaths: 1851, 18,934; 1852, 18,482; 1853, 20,301; 1854, 21,414; 1855, 20,798. Births: 1851, 28,681; 1852, 29,802; 1853, 30,920; 1854, 31,997; 1855, 32,845.

resident foreigners, Catholics, the rules of whose church will hereafter be shown to exercise an important influence in preventing the destruction of fœtal life. The conclusion cannot therefore well be avoided, that in these facts there exists the evident relation here intimated, of effects to cause.

With some certainty then, even though statistics are as yet so imperfect, can we assert this conclusion, that, frightful as is the extent to which the crime of abortion is perpetrated abroad,[1] there is reason to believe that it prevails to an equal, if not even greater, extent at home.

So far as we are aware, there has been no attempt made to invalidate the correctness of the above reasoning, during the years that have elapsed, since we first called the attention of statisticians to these startling and I believe unimpregnable factors.

Just as the present book is going to the press however, a friend, who, while acknowledging the truth of most of our premises, has yet felt a natural disinclination to accept their conclusions, directs our notice to a new point, important in this connection, but tending emphatically to support rather than to subvert our views. "One fact," writes this gentleman (to whom we have already referred), "is shown in Providence, and nowhere else. It is this, that the foreign mothers, mostly Catholic, have nearly twice as many still-born children, in proportion to the whole number, as the American mothers. Thus in 1864, 1 in 29.3 of all the children of American mothers were still-born, and 1 in 12.7 of the children of Irish mothers. In 1865, of American mothers, 1 in 18.1 still-born; of Irish mothers, 1 in 12.3. In 1866, of American mothers, 1 in 22.5; of Irish mothers, 1 in 14.4. Thus, including premature births, the Irish-

[1] A late number of the Pall-Mall Gazette, in an editorial, calls attention to the fact, that, while Dr. Farr, the Registrar-General, has announced that there are, in England and Wales alone, more than one million of childless families, other authorities affirm that the English race is so far less prolific than in former times, that, in their large towns, two children to each married couple has come to be the average number.

Catholic mothers have a far greater proportion of still-born children than the American-Protestant mothers." Now with reference to this fact, if the greater proportion of the still-births occurring were owing to accidental causes, we should expect to find, even upon so small a basis of computation as three years, that the proportion of still-births in Catholics and Protestants would hold some constant relation to itself in each class, if not to each other; whereas there is a range of no less than eleven per cent between the two American extremes given by Dr. Snow, while in the Catholic the range is only two per cent. The true explanation, however, lies in this: that in a certain proportion of cases, Protestant and Catholic, the labor is more or less impeded or complicated by a variety of causes, inherent or accidental; such as inertia of the womb, disproportion between the size of the fœtus and the diameters of the pelvis, &c., which, if unrelieved, prove fatal to the child, during or previous to its delivery, and in many instances to the mother also. Most, if not all, of these sources of danger are now amenable to proper medical treatment. In Protestant practice, the rule is to early assist nature, or, if necessary, to interfere with or correct her aberrations, as by turning the child *in utero*, or by applying the forceps, &c., and thus extracting it alive, when otherwise it must have died; while among Catholics, on the contrary, any such measures are almost invariably forbidden by the patient, her friends, or the clergy, lest the spiritual salvation of the fœtus should thereby be imperilled. To overcome these scruples, there is but a single course; to this we shall soon allude: it is a course, however, that has not yet been pursued to any extent by physicians in this country, and the fact remains as we have stated it. It is sufficient, we think, to afford a full explanation of our friend's problem.

3. The frequency of arrests or trials for abortion affords, save indirectly, no criterion of the actual frequency of the crime. Our laws on this subject are at present so easily

evaded, that officers of justice find it useless to trouble themselves with prosecution for the crime: it is indeed "*non poursuivie.*" During the eight years from 1849 to 1858, no report for 1853 being rendered by the Attorney-General, there were 32 trials for abortion in Massachusetts; and in these there was not a single conviction.[1] An estimate that for every arrest for this crime, a thousand instances of its commission escape the vigilance or at least the hand of the law, would probably be within the truth. That such is the fact, is shown by the statistics of France, where, from 1846 to 1850, out of 188 cases that came to the knowledge of the police, for lack of decisive evidence only 22 went to trial,[2] or about one-ninth of those legally investigated. From 1826 to 1853, there were in France 183 trials for abortion. At the above ratio, this will give about 1,700 cases judicially examined, a yearly average throughout the empire of between 50 and 60. Comparing this fact with the statistics of the Morgue already given, and with those of the actual decrease of the rate of increase of the population in Paris and in New York, and the increase of premature births, our statement of its frequency will not seem exaggerated.

4. The frequency of maternal deaths, confessedly from criminal abortion, as gathered from published statements and mortuary reports, is also an item of importance in our summary of evidence. It is probable that in but few of the fatal cases really occurring, is foul play ever thought of, especially if the standing of the victim, and her previous history, have been such as to prevent or disarm suspicion; and on the other hand, while immediate death is undoubtedly a frequent result of induced abortion, it is, in proportion to the cases of its later occurrence, or of confirmed and chronic ill-health resulting from the act, comparatively rare.

[1] Reports of Attorney-General of Massachusetts, from 1849 to 1858. State Documents.

[2] Comptes Rendus Annuels de la Justice Criminelle.

From which it must be granted that, for every case thus made known, very many others must necessarily exist.

5. The number and success of professed abortionists is notorious. If arrested, they are always ready with bribes or abundant bail. Hardly a newspaper throughout the land that does not contain their open and pointed advertisements, or a drug-store whose shelves are not crowded with their nostrums, publicly and unblushingly displayed: the supply of an article presupposes its demand. The profits that must be made from the sale of drugs supposed abortifacient may be judged from the extent to which they are advertised, and the prices willingly paid for them. From these facts, we may fairly estimate the extent of the nefarious traffic.

It is a comfort to believe that none of the alleged specifics possess directly the power attributed to them, their effect upon the womb, when produced, being of a secondary character, and dependent upon a severe disturbance, in itself very dangerous, of the adjacent intestinal canal. It is however, in equal degree, a grief to know that, even if unsuccessful in producing the effect for which they were designed, they frequently destroy the mother's life, and almost invariably, if she survive, her subsequent health.

6. That families are seldom now found of the size formerly common, is also a matter of general remark. It were foolish to attempt to explain this by supposing that the present is an age of more moderate desire, or less unbridled lust: there is too much collateral proof against any such plea. Nor is it reasonable to think that women are generally becoming less productive of offspring than formerly, from any natural cause; or that the mass of our population, whatever the exceptions, are already so far advanced in knowledge, physiological or mechanical, or in practice, as in most cases to be able to regulate impregnation at will.[1]

[1] We are sorry to be obliged to state that the knowledge above referred to is rapidly becoming universal. We have elsewhere pointed out the inevitable

The number of pregnancies must be nearly, if not quite, as abundant as formerly: who can doubt what becomes of the offspring? It is now acknowledged that, allowing for the effect of religious belief, to which we have already referred, and considering only the families of Protestants, we seldom find them containing as many children as formerly was the average. We have elsewhere shown that this is no matter of accident, nor decline in the general constitutional vigor of our people. However marked this change of constitution may seem, we believe it apparent rather than real, and owing to the fact that the so-called hardening process, to which the privations and exposures of our ancestors subjected them, destroyed many of their offspring in early years, just as obtains with savages and with lower animals. Thanks to the comforts of modern civilization, and the progress of medical science, these tenderlings are now saved, and reared to maturity. The late civil war proved most abundantly that neither the sires nor the sons of the present day are physically degenerate. We have shown, moreover, that our men are sexually as potent, when they choose to be, and our women naturally as fruitful as their predecessors; and that the sterility of the age is chiefly intentional, and not acquired. Dr. Allen, of Lowell, while admitting the frequency of criminal abortions, has endeavored to bridge this moral chasm on the supposition of a progressive constitutional change in American women, precluding them from conception, from carrying their children to maturity, or from safely giving them birth.[1]

detriment occasioned to parties of either sex by the systematic prevention of pregnancy, no matter in what way this may be accomplished.

[1] This theory, which, it need hardly be said, is not borne out by facts, Dr. Allen has stated at great length in a paper upon "The Law of Human Increase; or, Population based upon Physiology and Psychology," published in the New-York Journal of Psychological Medicine and Medical Jurisprudence, for April of the present year. The reasonings there offered do not reach the main question involved, as has been shown in the Boston Medical and Surgical Journal, for April 23.

As well assert that the present fashion of foregoing lactation, so prolific in causing uterine disease, were generally owing to absence of milk or of the mammary glands. Women still menstruate as well as ever they did, and, in consequence of advanced knowledge of their diseases by physicians, probably better. While the menstrual function lasts, and in the absence of distinct organic local disease, which is generally to be found when it exists, if searched for, women can conceive; that is, if their husbands are potent. Many of the more serious disturbances of pregnancy are now amenable to treatment; and, by the employment of anæsthesia, its greatest dangers have been removed from child-bed.

7. Of the experience of physicians, there can be but one opinion. If each man of the profession were honestly to investigate this matter, and as honestly to avow the result, the mass of evidence would be overwhelming. This statement is in no wise invalidated by the experience alleged by many, especially among older practitioners: their evidence, based chiefly on lack of inquisition, or on the acknowledged less prevalence of the crime in former years, is merely negative, and as such only to be valued.

"We blush," says Professor Hodge, "while we acknowledge the fact, that in this city [Philadelphia], where literature, science, morality, and Christianity, are supposed to have so much influence; where all the domestic and social virtues are reported as being in full and delightful exercise, even here" it prevails.[1]

The late Dr. Blatchford, of Troy, N.Y., wrote us thus: "A crime which forty years ago, when I was a young practitioner, was of rare and secret occurrence, has become frequent and bold." There is no need for us to multiply instances of what has long been the almost universal experience. To quote the forcible language, more expressive than elegant, of a New-Hampshire physician, "Nowadays,

[1] Introductory Lecture, 1854, p. 17.

if a baby accidentally finds a lodgement in the uterus, it may perchance have a knitting-needle stuck in its eyes before it has any."

Applications for abortion are in many neighborhoods of constant occurrence, by no means among the poorer classes alone; and few women, unless convinced by their physician of the enormity and guilt of that they intend, are deterred by his refusal from going elsewhere for aid, or from inducing abortion upon themselves.

But far greater proof than this we all possess, or can, if we desire. In but few of the abortions criminally induced is an application ever made to the physician in regular standing. He is oftener called upon, after the crime has already been committed, to treat its acute and immediate effects. If he choose to take for granted in every case, that it has occurred from a perfectly natural cause, even where attending circumstances clearly point to the contrary, or to ask no questions, or to shut his eyes and his ears to evident and patent facts, he can of course do so, and perhaps persuade himself that the crime is rare; but if he reflect that upon himself, more than on clergyman or legislator, rests the standard of public morals, and act accordingly, he may arrive at a different result.

But this is not only the fact in acute cases of abortion. The same statement holds true, perhaps even to a greater extent, with regard to chronic obstetric disease. It is now acknowledged that much of this is really the consequence of past difficult or abnormal labors; that the more complicated or improperly interfered with, the labor has been, the more certain are unfortunate sequelæ; and that the earlier in pregnancy its occurrence, the greater, as a general rule, the danger, not merely to the mother's life, but, if she survive, to her subsequent health. In the treatment of these results, even more marked perhaps at a late period than earlier, the dependence of effect on cause, and their evident connection, can often be learned by a faithful inquirer; and in no small proportion of cases does the history go back, without turn or the shadow of a doubt, to an induction of criminal abortion.

As a mere matter of individual experience, and from a practice by no means exceptional, the writer early in his practice reported no less than fifteen such cases as occurring to himself within a period of less than six months; and of these, all, without exception, were married and respectable women,[1] many of them of wealth and high social standing; and, subsequently, he was able, in consultation, to point out similar cases in the practice of gentlemen who, at that time, had denied the legitimacy of his conclusions. This experience must be a common one; only some lack the courage, as others lack the will, to investigate the matter: should they do so, they can come but to one result. Ten years ago, when we first broached this subject, physicians had a vague idea that unnecessary abortions were probably common: the fact has now been proved to more than a demonstration. Our medical journals teem with reported cases: our later text-books not only admit their occurrence, but call attention to it as one of the most decided causes of the so prevalent ill-health of the American women; while the American Medical Association considered the latter point of such importance, as an efficient argument against the crime, that it authorized the publication of its Prize Essay upon the subject—entitled "Why Not?"—for general circulation.

We are compelled, from the preceding considerations, to acknowledge, not merely that criminal abortion is of alarming frequency among us, but that its frequency is rapidly increasing; this having been made apparent by each link in the chain of evidence that has been presented. Every effort that might possibly check this flood of guilt will, if delayed, have so much the more to accomplish. The crime

[1] Report to Suffolk Dist. Med. Society, May, 1857; New-York Med. Gazette, July, 1857, p. 390; N.H. Journal of Medicine, July, 1857, p. 211.

is fast becoming, if it has not already become, an established custom, less honored in the breach than in the observance.[1]

What are the causes of this general turpitude?

They also may be classified: —

1. The low *morale* of the community as regards the guilt of the crime.

2. The doctrines of political economists.

3. The fear of child-bed.

4. The ease with which the character of the crime may, in individual cases, be concealed.

5. The unwillingness of its victims to give testimony that would also criminate themselves.

6. The possibility of their inducing abortion upon themselves without aid.

7. The ease with which the laws, as at present standing, may be evaded.

8. The lack or inefficacy of judicial preventives; such as

[1] Thus we wrote in 1859. Since then, though so great a flood of light has been poured upon the subject, the times seem little changed. Let us hope, however, that the apparent fact may be owing to the unveiling of what was formerly more frequently practised, but kept concealed. "The public prints, the National Medical Association, and the profession, have drawn the attention of the community to the melancholy frequency and comparative impunity which marks the practice of the abortionists. Still the daily press publishes the advertisements of these people in such thinly veiled language that the purport cannot be mistaken; while pregnant women are tempted to solicit such treatment by the necessity for concealing their shame, from ignorance of the vitality of the fœtus, and reluctance to incur the cares, risks, and responsibilities of maternity." ELLIOT, Obstetric Clinic, 1868, p. 383.

While these sheets are passing through the press, Professor GAILLARD THOMAS, of New York, has issued a most excellent work upon the Diseases of Women. In discussing the causes of these diseases, he corroborates all that we have urged for years concerning the fatal influences, and frequency, of criminal abortion, and closes his remarks upon this subject with the following words: "However much I may desire reformation in this matter, it is not in the spirit of a reformer that all this is written. I am not raising my voice against a great national crime, but am striving merely to establish the truth of my statement, that this crime is so frequent as to constitute in all classes of society, for it is limited to none, a great cause for uterine diseases." THOMAS, Practical Treatise on the Diseases of Women, 1868, p. 59.

statutes for registration, and those against concealment of birth and secret burials.

9. The prevalent ignorance of the true principles of its jurisprudence, in both government officials and medical witnesses.

10. Social extravagance and dissipation.

1. That public opinion should at present attach so little importance to the value of fœtal life, has already been shown to be owing in great measure to ignorance respecting its actual existence in the earlier months of pregnancy. Two other, and no less general, physiological errors prevail, extensively inculcated by popular authors and lecturers for their own sinister purposes.

One of these is the doctrine that it is detrimental to a woman's health to bear children beyond a certain number, or oftener than at certain stated periods, and that any number of abortions are not merely excusable, as preventives, but advisable;—it being entirely forgotten that the frequency of connection may be kept within bounds, and the times of its occurrence regulated, by those who are not willing to hazard its consequences;[1] that if women will, to escape trouble or for fashion's sake, forego the duty and privilege of nursing, a law entailed upon them by nature, and seldom neglected without disastrous results to their own constitutions, they must expect more frequent impregnation; that the habit of aborting is generally attended with the habit of more readily conceiving; and that abortions, accidental, and still more if induced, are generally attended by the loss of subsequent health, if not of life.

This error is one which would justify abortion as necessary for the mother's own good; a selfish plea. The other is based on a more generous motive. It is that the fewer one's

[1] As we have stated on a page just preceding, there are no means whatever of artificially preventing pregnancy, whether by imperfect intercourse or otherwise, that are not positively injurious to one or both of the parties engaged.

children, the more healthy they are likely to be, and the more worth to society. It is, however, equally fallacious with the first, and is without foundation in fact. The Spartans and Romans, so confidently appealed to, gave birth probably to as many weakly children as do our own women; that they destroyed many for this reason in infancy, is notorious. The brawny Highlanders are not the only offspring of their parents: the others cannot endure the national processes of hardening by exposure and diet, and so die young from natural causes. But were this theory true even so far as it goes, the world, our own country, could ill spare its frailer children, who oftenest, perhaps, represent its intellect and its genius.

2. In asserting that the doctrines of the leading political economists for the last half-century are accountable for much of the prevalence and increase of the crime, ignorant or careless as these writers all seem of the dire means that would be resorted to for the attainment of their ends, we have in no way exaggerated. Malthus remarks in his well-known Essay on Population, that "in the average state of a well-peopled territory, there cannot well be a worse sign than a large proportion of births, nor can there well be a better sign than a small proportion;"[1] and he indorses the assertion of Hume, subsequently proved false by Sadler,[2] that the permission of child-murder, by removing the fear of too numerous a family in case of marriage, tends to encourage this step, and thereby the increase of population; "the powerful yearnings of nature preventing parents from resorting to so cruel an expedient, except in extreme cases.[3]"

Sismondi[4] and a host of others might also be quoted; but a few extracts from a later writer, standard in this country

[1] Loc. cit., p. 313. [2] The Law of Population, 1830.

[3] Hume, Essays, vol. i. No. xi., p. 431.

[4] Etudes sur l'Economie Politique; Nouveaux Principes d'Economie Politique.

at present, and taught in our universities, till lately in that at Cambridge, for instance, will suffice.

"We greatly deprecate," says Mill, "an increase of population, as rapid as the increase of production and accumulation."[1]

"There is room in the world, no doubt, and even in old countries, for an immense increase of population. But although it may be innocuous, I confess I see very little reason for desiring it."

"I sincerely hope, for the sake of posterity, that they will be content to be stationary long before necessity compels them to it."[2]

"If the opinion were once generally established among the laboring class, that their welfare required a due regulation of the numbers of their families, only those would exempt themselves from it who were in the habit of making light of social obligations generally."[3] — "The principles contended for include not only the laboring classes, but all persons, except the few who, being able to give their offspring the means of independent support during the whole of life, do not leave them to swell the competition for employment."[4]

"When persons are once married, the idea never seems to enter any one's mind that having or not having a family, or the number of which it shall consist, is at all amenable to their own control. One would imagine that it was really, as the common phrases have it, God's will and not their own, which decided the number of their offspring."[5]

"In a place where there is no room left for new establishments," says Sismondi, entirely ignoring the escapes offered by emigration and the increased importation of food, "if a man has eight children, he should believe that, unless six of

[1] Loc. cit., ii. p. 253.

[2] Ibid., i. p. 451. An opinion to the same effect, italicized, has already been quoted.

[3] Ibid., ii. pp. 316, 317.

[4] Ibid., i. p. 452, foot-note.

[5] Ibid., i. p. 447.

them die in infancy, these, and three of his own contemporaries of each sex, will be compelled to abstain from marriage in consequence of his own imprudence."[1]

The direct result of remarks like these last, so pointed and plainly to be understood, is seen in the statistics we have so largely given. Would mankind, in following such advice, merely resort to greater abstinence before their means allow the expense of children, and to greater prudence after that period, no fault could be found; but when we discover criminal abortion thus justified and almost legitimated, we may well oppose to such doctrine the words of the indeed admirable Percival, "To extinguish the first spark of life is a crime of the same nature, both against our Maker and society, as to destroy an infant, a child, or a man."[2]

3. Fear of child-bed, in patients pregnant for the first time, or who had suffered or risked much in previous labors, might formerly have been allowed some weight in excuse, but none at all in these days of anæsthesia. It has been urged, and not so absurdly as would at first sight appear, that the present possibilities of painless and so much safer delivery, by changing thus completely the primal curse from anguish to a condition frequently of positive pleasure, remove a drawback of actual advantage, and, by offering too many inducements for pregnancy, tend to keep women in that state the greater part of their menstrual lives.

The consideration in detail of the various other causes to which we have alluded as accounting for the prevalence of abortion, together with that of the many special reasons offered in individual cases by way of excuse, we postpone for the present; merely premising that where ignorance is so evidently and so extensively its foundation, those who, possessing, yet withhold the knowledge which by any chance or in any way would tend to prevent it, themselves become, directly and in a moral sense, responsibly accountable for the crime.

[1] Nouveaux Principes, &c., liv. vii. ch. 5. [2] Medical Ethics, p. 79.

CHAPTER III.

ITS VICTIMS.

We have hitherto discussed abortion in the abstract, as a crime, and in its relations to the community at large. We have seen its heinous nature and its awful extent.

The division of the subject now to be examined, naturally presents itself under a fourfold aspect, — numerical, relational, social, and medical; representing respectively the multitude of the victims of abortion, their character as parent and child, their standing in the community, and the degree, whether unto death or otherwise, of their suffering.

So far as statistics will at present allow, the numerical relations of the victims of abortion have already been fully discussed, — the yearly thousands of fœtal and the frequent maternal deaths; one sacrifice at least, that of the child, being implied in every case.

Various incidental questions suggest themselves in this connection, curious, and by some, though erroneously, thought to be of judicial importance. Two of them will be here adverted to: they are the age of the mother and that of the fœtus.

It was formerly supposed, as in infanticide, that criminal abortion was seldom resorted to, save for the concealment of shame; and as seductions, confessedly frequent in comparison with adultery, are most common in the youth of women, it was laid down as probable that wilful abortions are most frequent between the years corresponding, from sixteen to twenty-five. Subsequent experience, however, has disproved this conclusion; and it is evident that the only real limit to their later occurrence is the menstrual climacteric, or so called turn of life. In many instances of marriage, abortions are resorted to at once; in others, after the family has reached a certain point, and are thence regularly continued.

The age of the fœtus is of much more interest; not, as will ultimately appear, for the same reason as in cases of infanticide, but as proving, to a certain extent, one of the facts we have already considered, — the error prevalent regarding the commencement of fœtal life.

It was Orfila's opinion, that criminal abortion was most frequent in the first two months of pregnancy. This would naturally have been supposed the case, as then some doubt might always obtain regarding its existence, and the excuse that the measures resorted to were for the purpose of preventing ill effect from an abnormal menstrual suppression would be more available. Devergie, on the other hand, was inclined to put the limits of greatest frequency at from three months to four and a half; while Briand and Chaudé thought the crime more common in the third month than the fifth, and in this last month much more frequent than even in the first or second. Tardieu also came to a similar conclusion.[1] He ascertained, that, of 34 cases investigated by himself, 25 were in from the third to the sixth month, and most of these in the third, 5 in the first two months, and 4 in the seventh and eighth; or that the cases in the third month, or shortly after, were five times as numerous as at either an earlier or a later period, and nearly three times as numerous as in both combined.

Upon examining the Register of the Parisian Morgue, we find its statistics strikingly corroborative of these deductions. We have already seen that from 1837–54 there had been deposited at the Morgue 692 fœtuses of less than nine months. Of these, 23 were from the first to the second month; 79 were from the second to the third; 108 were

[1] Annales d'Hygiène Publique, 1856, p. 122.

from the third to the fourth; 158 were from the fourth to the fifth; 150 were from the fifth to the sixth; 97 were from the sixth to the seventh; 48 were from the seventh to the eighth; and 29 were from the eighth to the ninth.

It has been stated, that 519, or five-sixths of them all, were not over six months; and it now appears, that, on a scale twenty times larger than that given by Tardieu from his own experience, nearly two-thirds of the fœtal deaths induced by abortion were in from the third to the sixth month of pregnancy; the three periods included giving a much larger proportion than any others, and the two last of them being almost identical. The extreme paucity shown by the above table in the first and nine months, and the decrease in the seventh and eighth from those preceding, are worthy of remark. It is probable that the sudden increase may be attributed to mental re-action after the first shock occasioned by the absolute certainty of pregnancy is past; and the subsequent decrease to the fact, that, in many attempted criminal abortions during the later months, children are born alive, the mother's courage then proving insufficient for infanticide and its more probable punishment, and her maternal affection being awakened by the sight of the child.

The truth seems to be, that while frequently the crime is committed in the very earliest period of pregnancy, in the belief that possibly all alarm may be false, in most cases the woman waits a month or two to be sure that she really is pregnant. After the sixth month, the comparative rarity of the crime is undoubtedly owing to the fact that fœtal life is then rendered certain by the movements of the child, which are perceived the more strongly as pregnancy advances.

It was formerly thought that the induction of criminal abortion was confined to the unmarried: there exists, however, abundant proof to the contrary. Had such been the fact, it would be reasonable to suppose, that, with the increase of marriages, the number of premature and still births would have lessened. In proportion, however, as the number of marriages has increased, so has the number of fœtal deaths, and in similar ratio the number of living births has declined; proving, as Husson was compelled to acknowledge of Paris, "a decrease in the fecundity of legitimate unions,"[1] explainable in no wise but by a criminal cause. Direct statistics on this point are still wanting, and must come almost entirely from medical men. The writer's published experience has been already referred to: subsequent practice has only confirmed it.

Again, the victims of abortion are not confined to the inhabitants of cities. Of the prosecutions in France during 1851–53, it appears that but little more than a tenth of the whole number occurred in the Department of the Seine.[2] But we have already furnished much stronger evidence on this point.

Finally, though the excessive extravagance of the day, entailing as it does to so many an annual expenditure incommensurate with their income, is accountable in no small degree for the crime, yet it cannot always be alleged. There is too much reason to believe that with our communities it is as with others. In France it appears that the poor and uneducated have on the whole the largest families, contrary in some respects to established hygienic rules; while, on the other hand, the rich are inclined, as far as possible, to restrict the number of their children, often, indeed, stipulating beforehand, at marriage or previously, that such shall be few or none,[3] as, indeed, we have repeatedly known to occur amongst our own upper classes. In every case that has come to our knowledge, this arrangement has resulted in unhappiness to both parties, and in several instances has led to divorce. If a man treat his wife as a strumpet, even

[1] Les Consummations, &c. [2] Comptes Rendus Annuels, &c.

[3] MAYER, Des Rapports Conjugaux, considérés sous le triple point de vue de la population, de la santé et de la morale publique, Paris, 1857.

at her own solicitation, unfaithfulness in one or the other is almost sure to result.

But not only must we believe that this crime prevails in our midst to an almost incredible extent among the wealthy and educated and married: we are compelled to admit, that Christianity itself, or at least Protestantism, has failed to check the increase of criminal abortion. It is not astonishing to find that the crime was known in ancient times, as shown by evidence previously given, nor that it exists at the present day among savage tribes, excused by ignorance and superstition; but that Christian communities should especially be found to tolerate and to practise it, does almost exceed belief.

In the previous remarks, the French have been compared with our own people, not merely because of their published statistics, but because, from their loose morals and habits of life, they might be thought to represent the extreme to which the crime would be likely to obtain among civilized nations. We have shown reason to suppose that we equal them in guilt, if we do not exceed them. Now, it must be borne in mind that the French are Catholic, and that the rules of that church do not, as has been generally supposed, permit abortion in the earlier months,[1] but that they rigidly exercise over fœtal life throughout pregnancy the most absolute guard and supervision;[2] instances of this, in cases where craniotomy is supposed to be indicated, are familiar to every medical practitioner. The church, here omnipotent against the physician, and desiring that every created human being should receive the benefit of baptism, demands that

[1] Cangiamila, Embryologia Sacra, p. 15.

[2] In verification of this statement, we are enabled to quote from a late authorized edition of the Canon Laws of the Church of Rome: Omnes, qui abortûs seu fœtûs immaturi, tam animati quam inanimati, formati vel informis, ejectionem procuraverint, pœnas propositas et inflictas tam divino quam humano jure, ac tam per canonicas sanctiones et apostolicas constitutiones quam civilia jura adversus veros homicidas incurrere, hâc nostrâ perpetuo valiturâ constitutione statuimus et ordinamus. Reiffenstuell, Jus Canonicum Universum, tome iii. Paris, 1854.

fœtal death must have taken place previously to the operation proposed. It does not seek for the signs of fœtal life, but takes this for granted, and requires that its absence must be proved before allowing the removal of the child, even though this is necessary to save the mother's life.

The rule runs thus: "Sedulam operam dent sacerdotes, ut quantum poterunt, impediant nefandum illud scelus quo adhibitis chirurgicis instrumentis infans in utero interficitur. Omnis fœtus quocumque tempore gestationis editus baptizetur, vel absolute, si constet de vitâ; vel sub conditione, nisi evidenter pateat eum vitâ carere."[1]

In cases where instrumental delivery is absolutely necessary, the ceremony of baptism as ordinarily administered is of course impossible. But as this is deemed so important by the Catholic Church,[2] even to the sacrifice of the mother, any means of overcoming this obstacle, fatal to countless maternal lives, should be accounted, if found practicable, of the utmost importance. For this purpose, therefore, we do not hesitate to recommend intra-uterine baptism; the consecrated element being carried to the child, if too high to be reached by the hand, by a sponge and staff, or, if necessary, by a syringe, as was long ago sanctioned by the theologists of the Sorbonne;[3] in the absence of a clergyman, if

1 Decreta Synodi plenariæ Episcoporum Hiberniæ, apud Thurles habitæ anno 1850; Art. de Baptismo, p. 20.

2 Dublin Review, April, 1858, p. 100.

3 Deventer, 1734, p. 366; Sterne, Tristram Shandy, p. 54; Med. Times and Gazette, Aug. 1858, p. 196. Though the fact of this decision has been doubted, it is nevertheless strictly true. Through the kindness of the late Bishop Fitzpatrick, we were favored with a copy of Barry's Medico-Christian Embryology, as presenting upon this point the authorized and generally received doctrine of the Catholic Church. We quote the following from the chapter "On Baptism in Impracticable and Difficult Labors:" —

"In case of impacted head, and at all times that one is obliged to apply the forceps, whether at one of the straits or in the pelvic excavation, it becomes necessary to baptize the child on the part which presents at the uterine orifice after the rupture of the bag containing the waters.

"In order to baptize the child, a syringe charged with natural water may be used. If this be not at hand, a person may use a sponge, or a linen or cotton rag, wetted with water, which is to be carried to the child by the

the case is urgent, the rite accounted so sacred being performed by the physician in attendance rather than to allow the death of the mother. We know that many of the profession, from fear of ridicule or dislike to sanction what they do nôt believe in, would shrink from such a duty. Is it not, however, due to humanity in every way to prevent this frequent murder? for such, by our apathy and neglect, the mother's death in these cases becomes. Can we, as Christians, refuse *any* aid? We are not ashamed to acknowledge, that for ourself, though no Catholic, we have repeatedly performed this intra-uterine baptism, where delivery without mutilation was impossible, or where other instrumental assistance became necessary. We could neither conscientiously assert the child's death, nor allow the mother to linger till it should occur, while the friends, in the absence of a priest, whose presence it was impossible to procure for many hours, would not permit the operation. Remonstrance was useless; had we refused we should have been morally responsible for the almost inevitable death of the woman: it was, therefore, simply our duty.

We shall now quote from an admirable letter we received from the late Catholic Bishop of Boston. The extracts are couched in so forcible language, and their spirit is so thoroughly Christian, that we need not apologize for their length, or that they recapitulate arguments we have already advanced.

"The doctrine of the Catholic Church," remarked Bishop Fitzpatrick, "her canons, her pontifical constitutions, her theologians, without exception, teach, and constantly have taught, that the destruction of the human fœtus in the

fingers, a pair of forceps, or any other suitable contrivance, and then squeezed or pressed on the surface of the part presenting." (Loc. cit., p. 45.)

"Any person, whether man, woman, or child, may baptize an infant when in danger of death." (Ibid., p. 76.)

If the facts now stated should be more generally known and acted upon by the medical profession, hundreds of lives, infant and maternal, now lost, would annually be saved.

womb of the mother, *at any period from the first instant of conception*, is a heinous crime, equal at least, in guilt, to that of murder. We find it distinctly condemned as such even as far back as the time of Tertullian (at the end of the second century), who calls it *festinatio homicidii*, a hastening of murder. The Pope, Sixtus the Fifth, in a bull published in 1588, subjects those guilty of the crime to all the penalties, civil and ecclesiastical, inflicted on murderers. It is denounced and reprobated in many other canons of the church.

"The reason of this doctrine (apart from the authority of the church) must, it seems to me, appear evident upon a little reflection. The very instant conception has taken place, there lies the vital germ of a man. True, it is hidden in the darkness of the womb, and it is helpless; but it has sacred rights, founded in God's law, so much the more to be respected because it is helpless. It may be already a living man, for neither mothers nor physicians can tell when life is infused; they can only tell when its presence is manifested, and there is a wide difference between these two things. At any rate, it is from the first moment potentially and *in radice* a man, with a body and a soul destined most surely, by the will of the Creator and by his law, to be developed into the fulness of human existence. No one can prevent that development without resisting and annulling one of the most sacred and important laws established by the Divine Author of the universe; and he is a criminal, a murderer, who deals an exterminating blow to that incipient man, and drives back into nothingness a being to whom God designed to give a living body and an immortal soul.

"From this it follows, that the young woman whose virtue has proved an insufficient guardian to her honor, when she seeks by abortion to save in the eyes of man that honor she has forfeited, incurs the additional and deeper guilt of murder in the eyes of God, the Judge of the living and the dead. Who can express what follows with regard to those women who, finding themselves lawfully mothers, prefer to devastate with poison or with steel their wombs, rather than bear the discomforts attached to the privilege of maternity, rather than forego the gayeties of a winter's balls, parties, and plays; or the pleasures of a summer's trips and amusements?

"But abortion," the Bishop continued, "besides being a direct crime against a positive law of God, is also an indirect crime against society. Admit its practice, and you throw open a way for the most unbridled licentiousness; you make woman a mere instrument for beastly lust. Every woman is somebody's mother or daughter or sister or wife; or she bears all these relations at once. Whatever protection, therefore, we would claim for a woman because she stands in any of these relations to us, we should also extend to all women, because they bear some one of all these relations to others. Most assuredly, then, we should remove none of the safeguards that protect female virtue. But, if we take away the responsibility of maternity, we destroy one of its strongest bulwarks.

"It affords me pleasure," he concluded, "to learn that the American Medical Association has turned its attention to the prevention of criminal abortion, a sin so directly opposed to the first laws of nature, and to the designs of God, our Creator, that it cannot fail to draw down a curse upon the land where it is generally practised." [1]

"Whenever the parents of the child," says Professor Elliot, "are Roman Catholics, and believe that baptism of the unborn child is essential, the operator should see that the presenting part of a living child be baptized before a dangerous operation is undertaken, since, according to the Roman Catholic Church, this can be done by a layman; and it is the duty of the physician to respect the religious conviction of his patients. This advice is desirable in this country, where all varieties of religious creeds are found, and enjoy an

[1] MS. Letter, dated Nov. 14, 1858.

equal independence."[1] It is almost needless to refer to the fact, that, among the lower classes, the rite should not be too indiscriminately resorted to. Depaul, for instance, relates a case where baptism was administered by the over-obliging physician to the child of Jewish parents, to the great grief of all parties concerned.

Such being the doctrine of the Catholic Church, and statistics nevertheless proving that its so stringent statutes against the destruction of fœtal life, enforced alike by denouncement and excommunication, are constantly broken in Catholic France, it is more than probable, from the existence of this fact, in addition to all the various causes of the crime we have seen equally prevailing there and in this country, that the actual number of abortions is much greater with ourselves; at least with the American and native portion of our population. We have, indeed, shown that this is really the case in Massachusetts.[2]

[1] ELLIOT, Obstetric Clinic, 1868, p. 17.

[2] It is not, of course, intended to imply, that Protestantism, as such, in any way encourages, or indeed permits, the practice of inducing abortion: its tenets are uncompromisingly hostile to all crime. So great, however, is the popular ignorance regarding this offence, that an abstract morality is here comparatively powerless; our American women arrogate to themselves the settlement of what they consider, if doubtful, purely an ethical question; and there can be no doubt, that the Romish ordinance, flanked on the one hand by the confessional, and by denouncement and excommunication on the other, has saved to the world thousands of infant lives.

During the ten years that have passed since the preceding sentence was written, we have had ample verification of its truth. Several hundreds of Protestant women have personally acknowledged to us their guilt, against whom only seven Catholics; and, of these, we found, upon further inquiry, that all but two were only nominally so, not going to the confession. The two referred to had each had some dozen children within fourteen or fifteen years, and thought that they had therefore a certain measure of excuse in desiring to rest awhile from their labors.

Since the last chapter went to the press, and within the past twenty-four hours, we have received the Annual Report of the City Registrar of Boston, for the year 1867. The following extracts will serve to corroborate the evidence that we have already adduced: "During the year 1867, there has been only one birth in each 34.78 of the population, estimating the latter at 205,000. In 1851, the births were in the ratio of one in 26 of the population; and since that year the birth-rate has been diminishing, until it has reached

Viewing this subject in a medical light, we find that death, however frequent, is by no means the most common or the worst result of the attempts at criminal abortion. This statement applies not to the mother alone, but, in a degree, to the child.

We shall perceive that many of the measures resorted to are by no means certain of success, often, indeed, decidedly inefficacious in causing the immediate expulsion of the fœtus from the womb, though almost always producing more or less severe local or general injury to the mother, and often, directly or by sympathy, to the child.

The membranes or placenta may be but partially detached, and the ovum may be retained. This does not necessarily occasion degeneration, as into a mole or hydatids, or entire arrest of development. The latter may be partial, as, under many forms, from some cause or another, does constantly occur. If from an usuccessful attempt at abortion, would this be confessed, or indeed always suggest itself to the mother's own mind? Fractures of the fœtal limbs prior to birth are often reported, unattributable in any way to the funis, which may amputate indeed, but seldom break a limb. A fall or a blow is recollected; perhaps it was accidental, perhaps not, for resort to these for criminal purposes is very common.

its present low state, with plain indications of falling still lower" (p. 3). "The number of children born in 1867, whose parents were both native born, was 24.11 per cent of the whole number of births. On the other hand, in those cases where both parents were foreign born, the number of births was 61.37 per cent of the whole number. When it is remembered that the population of Boston is very evenly divided between the foreign and the native born, the facts tabulated above bear an unpleasant aspect, and show, that, if there be any thing reprehensible in the undesirable result witnessed, it unmistakably belongs to the native population" (p. 4). "Not the least interesting fact connected with this subject is, that the diminishing birth-rate affects principally the native population; and, as this result does not vary essentially from year to year, the malady seems, therefore, not only chronic, but points unmistakably in the direction where it is seated. . . . The subject is one of vast importance, and its bearing upon the vital interests of the community can scarcely be over-estimated" (pp. 36, 37).

In precisely the same manner may injury be occasioned to the nervous system of the fœtus, as in a hydrocephalic case long under the writer's own observation, where the cause and effect were plainly evident. Intra-uterine convulsions have been reported; as induced by external violence, they are probably not uncommon, and the disease thus begun may eventuate in epilepsy, paralysis, or idiocy.

To the mother there may happen correspondingly frequent and serious results. Not alone death, immediate or subsequent, may occur, from metritis, hemorrhage, peritonitic or phlebitic inflammation, from almost every cause possibly attending, not merely labor at the full period, comparatively safe, but miscarriage, — increased and multiplied by ignorance, by wounds and violence; but, if life still remain, it is too often rendered worse than death.

The results of abortion from natural causes, as obstetric disease, separate or in common, of mother, fœtus, or membranes, or from a morbid habit consequent on its repetition, are much worse than those following the average of labors at the full period. If the abortion be from accident, from external violence, mental shock, great constitutional disturbance from disease or poison, or even necessarily induced by the skilful physician in early pregnancy, the risks are worse. But if, taking into account the patient's constitution, her previous health and the period of gestation, the abortion has been criminal, these risks are infinitely increased.[1] Those who escape them are few.[2]

[1] PASSOT, Des Dangers de l'Avortement provoqué dans un But Criminel. Gazette Méd. de Lyon, 1853.

[2] At the time that we first expressed our own opinion upon this matter, there were many physicians who were apparently unaware of the true state of the case. Since then, however, much corroborative evidence has been put upon record, latest by Professor FORDYCE BARKER, of New York, who says: "The prognosis is particularly grave in abortion caused by criminal means. The dangers from hemorrhage may be either from a sudden gush, or a continued leakage, or recurring hemorrhages, due to retained placenta or membranes. From the same cause may arise peritonitis, septicæmia, &c. Other results are moles, subinvolution of the uterus, and sterility. As

In thirty-four cases of criminal abortion reported by Tardieu, where the history was known, twenty-two were followed, as a consequence, by death, and only twelve were not. In fifteen cases necessarily induced by physicians, not one was fatal.[1]

It is a mistake to suppose, with Devergie, that death must be immediate, and owing only to the causes just mentioned. The rapidity of death, even where directly the consequence, greatly varies; though generally taking place almost at once if there be hemorrhage, it may be delayed even for hours where there has been great laceration of the uterus, its surrounding tissues, and even of the intestines;[2] if metro-peritonitis ensue, the patient may survive for from one to four days, even indeed to seven and ten. But there are other fatal cases, where on autopsy there is revealed no appreciable lesion; death, the penalty of unwarrantably interfering with nature, being occasioned by the entrance of a bubble of air into the circulation through a severed utero-placental vessel,[3] and by syncope, by excess of pain, or by moral shock from the thought of the crime.[4]

That abortions, even when criminally induced, may sometimes be safely borne by the system, is of little avail to disprove the evidence of numberless cases to the contrary. We have instanced death. Pelvic cellulitis, on the other hand; fistulæ, vesical, uterine, or between the organs alluded

compared with delivery at the full term, abortion may not be immediately so dangerous, but it is later much worse. If cases of puerperal fever in hospitals are excluded, more deaths occur from abortion than from delivery at full time." (New-York Med. Gazette, 8 Feb. 1868, p. 154.)

[1] Ann. d'Hygiène, 1856, p. 147.

[2] Dubois and Devergie, Ibid. tome xix. p. 425; tome xxxix. p. 157.

[3] A case of this kind is detailed by Dr. Hitchcock, of Kalamazoo, Mich. The abortionist, having separated a portion of the fœtal membranes from the uterine wall by a catheter, blew a puff of air through the instrument to still farther detach them. The patient threw up her arms, and immediately expired. (Transactions of the American Medical Association, 1864, p. 83.) For further illustrations in point, see Reid, Physiological Researches, p. 578; Simpson, Obstetric Works, vol. i. p. 719.

[4] Dubois and Devergie, loc. cit.

to; adhesions of the os uteri or vagina, rendering liable subsequent rupture of the womb, during labor or from retained menses, or, in the latter case, discharge of the secretion through a Fallopian tube and consequent peritonitis; diseases and degenerations, inflammatory or malignant, of both uterus and ovary; of this long and fearful list, each, too frequently incurable, may be the direct and evident consequence, in one patient or another, of an intentional and unjustifiable abortion.

We have seen, that, in some instances, the thought of the crime, coming upon the mind at a time when the physical system is weak and prostrated, is sufficient to occasion death. The same tremendous idea, so laden with the consciousness of guilt against God, humanity, and even mere natural instinct, is undoubtedly able, where not affecting life, to produce insanity.

This it may do either by its first and sudden occurrence to the mind, or, subsequently, by those long and unavailing regrets, that remorse, if conscience exist, is sure to bring. The mental aberration may also be produced, and undoubtedly frequently is, by the reflex cerebral irritation induced by either of the pelvic lesions, that we have instanced as directly resulting from abortion.[1] Were we wrong in considering death the preferable alternative?

[1] To the decided effect, akin to neuralgia, very frequently produced upon the mental system by uterine and ovarian disease, we have had occasion to direct the attention of the medical profession. (Boston Med. and Surg. Journal, April, Oct. and Nov. 1864; Transactions of the American Med. Association, 1865, p. 125, &c.) Inasmuch as several of the gentlemen charged with the supervision of our lunatic hospitals have been slow to apply towards the cure of their patients the practical suggestions that we have made, the evidence lately afforded by one of their own number upon the causation of insanity by abortion will be read with interest. "I have for many years," says Dr. Gray, of the New-York State Asylum at Utica, "received and treated patients whose insanity was directly traceable to this crime through its moral and physical effects." And again: "I need not here discuss at length the disorders consequent upon this crime in any and all of its shades; but I deem it no less than my duty to declare, as already stated, that it is directly and indirectly one of the causes of insanity." (Twenty-fourth Annual Report of the New-York State Lunatic Asylum, 1867.)

CHAPTER IV.

ITS PROOFS.

It is by no means an easy thing in all cases to obtain evidence that an abortion has occurred; still more difficult, that it has been intentionally induced. As most laws read, it is necessary at the outset to prove the existence of pregnancy; as many still stand, it must be shown that the woman has quickened. These requisitions are unwise and unjust; and under them, if insisted on by adroit counsel, it is almost useless to pursue prosecution. In the earlier months, before quickening has occurred or the fœtal pulsations have become evident to the ear, it is impossible, as we have elsewhere insisted,[1] ever to be sure of the existence of pregnancy; and yet attempts at its termination are then in no degree less criminal. The only infallible sign of pregnancy is the sound of the fœtal heart, not always to be detected, even by the double stethoscope.[2]

Putting aside, therefore, the question of the existence of pregnancy and of fœtal life, as taken for granted, on the one hand, by the attempt at their termination, and as proved, on the other, by this result, it is found that the evidence of abortion classifies itself into proofs of its occurrence, of its commission, of the criminal intent, and of the identity of the party accused.

[1] Review of Montgomery's Signs of Pregnancy, North-American Medico-Chirurgical Review, March, 1857, p. 249.

[2] It is unnecessary for us to go into discussion of the relative value of the signs of pregnancy. The works of Montgomery and other writers upon this special point, and, indeed, most text-books upon common midwifery, afford all the detail that is likely to be required. It is, of course, very important, here as elsewhere, that only the latest editions of any author be cited or allowed to be recognized in court.

1. *The Occurrence.*

The abortion may perhaps be known to have taken place by confession or witness; in either case requiring no further demonstration. Instances are not rare, however, where suspicion merely may exist, and the fact must be proved by collateral testimony; and this in two cases,— where the woman is still alive, and where she is dead.

The general history of the case, even if pregnancy and delivery be equally denied, may throw some light on its true nature. This as given, no matter how affected by the evidence of interested or implicated witnesses, may be probable or improbable; as in an instance related by Burns,[1] where her sudden lessening in bulk was ascribed by a patient to a night's profuse sweating, of course an impossible result. But, on the other hand, care is necessary, lest, from its rarity of occurrence or its improbability, the reality should be disbelieved. Cases are on record where innocent women, suffering from retention of menses or from ovarian disease, and suddenly relieved by a critical and spontaneous discharge, have, on suspicion of abortion, lost character and even their lives. If a woman's statements should contradict each other, this fact of itself may reveal the truth.

There are at times difficulties in proving delivery at the full period of pregnancy, as is well known. The earlier in gestation, if the patient survive, the more these difficulties are enhanced. The occurrence of normal labor cannot be discovered with any certainty by a personal examination after eight days have elapsed;[2] those of an early abortion, not even after only one or two.[3] The signs of delivery that are well marked at the full period, the general symptoms then

1 Principles of Midwifery, p. 547.

2 Baudelocque, tome i. p. 115; Fodere, ii. p. 17; Marc, Dict. de Méd., i. p. 228; Montgomery, Signs of Pregnancy, p. 578; Devergie, Méd. Légale, i. p. 244.

3 Ryan, p. 267; Tardieu, loc. cit.

obtaining, the size of the uterus, ascertained by a combined use of the hand and the uterine sound, lacerations of the perineum and cervix uteri, the presence of the lochia, the state of the breasts, abdomen, vagina, and vulva, all of little value except in conjunction with each other, are proportionately less defined as we go back in time, until, near the commencement of pregnancy, it becomes impossible to distinguish an abortion from an attack of severe hemorrhage or from menorrhagia, unless by detecting the impregnated ovum. Even in cases where it would seem that there could be no doubt whatever of the fact, the worst error might yet occur; for, in what is called membranous dysmenorrhœa, the mucous membrane lining the uterine cavity is thrown off, either entire or in shreds, greatly hypertrophied, and the dysmenorrhœal pains attending its expulsion may so closely similate those of an abortion as to deceive even a wary physician. The regularity of these attacks, usually occurring at every menstrual period, serves as an important element of diagnosis. We have shown, moreover, that it is possible in some cases of uterine disease innocently acquired, as cancer, to be deceived by the impression given to the touch upon digital examination, and to form the erroneous opinion that the case is one of induced abortion.

If the patient is dead, and too long time have not elapsed since the supposed occurrence of the crime, decision is often more easy; many facts in the case being generally known, and concealment being less possible. If the ovum, but partially detached, be still retained, the fact may be self-evident; for, if the embryo be present, its envelopes cannot be confounded with the dysmenorrhœal membrane, to which we have just referred; if it has been discharged, and concealed or lost, there will still be present the recent corpus luteum,[1]

[1] The corpus luteum, so called, of pregnancy, as distinguished from that of mere menstruation, is no longer to be relied upon. For a discussion of this question, see the later text-books on physiology, as those of Dalton and Austin Flint, Jr.

and other well-known signs, in proportion to the period of the pregnancy. Allowance, in this latter respect, must be made for the possibility of partial uterine contraction after death, as is sometimes known to occur at the full period;[1] the writer has seen it to a marked degree, some time previous to the expiration of pregnancy, at a Cæsarean section, after death from laryngitis, occurring in the Edinburgh Maternity Hospital in 1854.

2. *The Commission.*

Allowing the fact of the occurrence of an abortion to be proved or granted, it becomes necessary to discover its cause, whether accidental, natural, or intentional; and, in the latter case, whether it were justifiable or criminal. Of this it will be found that the proofs are both positive and negative; drawn from the history of the case and from personal examination of the patient and the fœtus. The value of each of these elements is increased in proportion as it is compared with the other; but "this I wish most especially to have noted, that WHEREVER THERE IS A MISCARRIAGE, THERE IS ALWAYS PRESENT SOME ACTUAL, PERCEPTIBLE, AND OFTEN TANGIBLE CAUSE."[2]

The story of the patient may be to one effect, and that of other parties involved to a very different one; if the first is corroborated by the second, it may again, as has already been remarked, present or not present the likelihood of truth. If the habit of aborting at a certain period has existed, which of course cannot be alleged in a first pregnancy; if the patient has had sudden fright or grief, or is known to have been accidentally injured,—the chances are to be considered in her favor, in the absence of proof to the

[1] CLARKE, Trans. of Soc. for Impr. of Med.-Chir. Knowledge, iii. p. 290; BAUDELOCQUE, i. p. 123, note; LEROUX, Traité des Pertes, Obs. xiii. p. 25; MONTGOMERY, loc. cit., p. 618.

[2] GARDNER, of New York, note to TYLER SMITH'S Lectures on Obstetrics, p. 203.

contrary. The converse of this statement, however, must not be considered as always and necessarily true. Women have time and again suffered shipwreck, undergone torture, been thrown from a height, and otherwise severely injured, and yet have escaped miscarriage;[1] while, on the other hand, they may repeatedly have aborted before, and yet, passing safely their usually critical point, may without trouble go on to the full period. In still other cases, there may exist local disease, pelvic or uterine, which, if left alone, would of itself occasion miscarriage; and the more decidedly do so, if accidentally or intentionally interfered with.

The character of the abortion is not without its value, whether occurring suddenly and without apparent cause, or preceded by maternal disease or the signs of fœtal death.

Examination of the mother, though proof that she has herself been injured is not necessary to establish the crime, may reveal local wounds and mutilations; or their absence, which, however, by no means goes to prove that violence may not have been inflicted; and, on the other hand, as in a case once reported by the writer to the Boston Society for Medical Observation, traces of former violence in instrumental or other labors may remain, and to such an extent

[1] This is a very important matter, the true explanation of which up to this time (1868) seems hardly to have been given. It is, however, simple enough. The ordinary term of pregnancy expires at the end of nine calendar months and a week, or ten lunar months; that is to say, labor normally occurs at the tenth menstrual period. Now, at every menstrual period during pregnancy, there is a slight molimen, or effort at the re-establishment of the catamenial discharge. This in some women is so marked as to result in a hemorrhage from the external surface of the neck of the womb, giving rise at times to the belief that pregnancy cannot be present. Now in all cases, whether or no any signs of local or constitutional disturbance be noticed, there is probably a greater tendency to miscarry at these times than during the intervals; and hence it is, that a woman who has perhaps undergone some severe shock, as of a railroad accident or a surgical operation, at one period of her pregnancy with impunity, may at another abort upon the most trifling provocation. These considerations are of the very greatest value, not merely to medical jurists, but to those engaged in the practice of medicine.

as to give to the touch every character of a recent and criminal interference.[1] The fœtus may show pre-existing and natural disease sufficient to account for the effect apparent, or may present the signs of direct and intentional interference. Recent scars of venesection on the arms and feet, or of leech-bites, especially on the upper and inner parts of the thighs, and vesications upon the breasts, are suspicious in a patient who has aborted, unless they were evidently required by the state of her previous health. If signs of irritant injections into the vagina are present, they are ground for more than suspicion; but these must not be confounded with the effects of ordinary disease or measures for their relief. Severe inflammation of the rectum very often, perhaps usually, results from the employment of the drastic pills so largely advertised as specifics. These, almost all of them, contain aloes as their chief ingredient, and act upon the uterus only secondarily, by establishing a sympathetic inflammation of that organ. The rectal inflammation may, however, be simply hemorrhoidal and chronic in its character, just as the metritis or uterine inflammation may be, and often is, found in virgins who have never been touched by men; the disturbance being induced by a great variety of causes, as exertion, or taking cold while the menses are present, &c.

The instrument, where used, with which the operation has been performed, may sometimes be identified; though this is almost impossible, unless by confession or direct testimony. The weapons resorted to by the unprofessional are various; knitting-needles, pen-handles, skewers, goose-

[1] In the instance referred to, the cervix uteri had been deeply and extensively lacerated, forceps having been used in four previous labors; while depressions existing between the old cicatrices, and ragged and half filled with clots, were decidedly suggestive of punctured wounds. (Am. Journ. of the Med. Sciences, April, 1859.) The true nature of the case was rendered evident by its past history, and corroborated by the fact that the patient was a Catholic; the latter being a point to which we are inclined to attach much importance, for reasons already given.

quills, pieces of whale-bone, and even curtain-rods, are among the number. The finger alone, except where the uterus is prolapsed or can be depressed, and the os is very soft and patulous, is seldom, if ever, sufficient for the deed. If a physician be accused, it is important to notice with what instrument the crime is said to have been performed, whether this was before witnesses, and whether it was introduced openly or under pretence of a digital examination.[1]

The sensations of the patient at the time are also, in different cases, unlike each other. In some instances, nothing unusual is observed; in others, a prick or probing; but in most, an acute and tearing uterine pain, often followed by syncope or an hysterical attack. These sensations however, it must be borne in mind, are very often present, especially in hysterical subjects, during an ordinary vaginal examination for uterine disease, even if nothing whatever is employed in the way of treatment. Slight but immediate hemorrhage generally occurs, save in professional cases, during the attempt at abortion; and it is usually increased by compelled exercise, prolonged baths, or ergot.

The time ensuing before the expulsion of the fœtus is an element not to be lost sight of. In 34 cases reported by Orfila, the minimum observed was 13½ hours, the maximum 6 days; in 36 cases by Tardieu, the minimum was 5 hours, the maximum 11 days. Of these last cases, however, 29 were within 4 days.

It cannot be alleged in excuse, that the sex of the child,

[1] Some physicians consider it proper, when legitimately treating uterine disease, to conceal from their patients the details of all the treatment pursued, in order to prevent anxiety, and other excitement of the nervous system. We are inclined, however, to believe, that here as elsewhere honesty is the best policy. The patient, and certainly some near friend of hers, can be told what is being done, without undue and unprofessional exaggeration of its nature, or creating alarm; and frankness of this kind, on the part of an attendant, always begets increased confidence in his reliability and good judgment.

so fatal both to itself and the mother in many instances of advanced pregnancy,[1] has any influence in producing early abortion. In 293 premature still-births reported by Collins,[2] 146 were male and 147 female, bearing the proportion of 100 to 100. Nor can the plea of Drs. Gordon Smith, Good, Paris, and Copeland, that as a fœtus born before the seventh month has a slender chance of surviving, its murder should be viewed with leniency,[3] be allowed. Such arguments, that the perils and dangers to which the fœtus is naturally subjected should lessen the criminality of attempts at its destruction, are without foundation, and, when advanced by physicians, are utterly unworthy the profession.

3. *The Intent.*

We shall hereafter discuss the perpetrators of the crime, and the emergencies which can alone justify the induction of premature labor or obstetric abortion. We shall see that by none save medical men can such necessity ever be known; it is, therefore, apparent that the intent may frequently be judged from the relation of the parties implicated, and the excuses offered by them. It will also often appear from the other circumstances of the case. That the child was likely to be born a bastard, and to be chargeable to the reputed father, would be evidence to that effect; and proof of the clandestine manner in which the drugs, if such were used, were procured or administered, would tend the same way.[4]

On the part of the mother, bastardy also, the having denied the existence of pregnancy, concealed its expelled product, expressed an intention or desire to abort, made a known application for this purpose, visited a notorious abortionist, taken alleged specifics, or given similar advice to a friend, are all presumptive evidence; as are also the

[1] Simpson, Obstetric Works, i. p. 397.
[2] Practical Treatise, p. 275.
[3] Ryan, Med. Jurisprudence, p. 282.
[4] Roscoe, Ev. 242.

having neglected to send for aid when needed, or refused to take precautions or remedies when prescribed. In like manner, evidence of criminal intent would seem apparent, if drugs generally supposed abortive had been advised or given to a pregnant woman, or violence of any kind usually productive of the effect in question, even to tooth-drawing,[1] had been hastily or unnecessarily used.

Here, as in many other cases where no malice is expressed or openly indicated, the law will imply it; if, for instance, a man wilfully poisons another, in such a deliberate act the law presumes malice, though no particular enmity can be proved. Malice is not confined in its legal definition to ill-will toward one or more individual persons, but is intended to denote an action flowing from any wicked or corrupt motive, — a thing done *malo animo*, where the fact has been attended with such circumstances as carry in them the plain indications of a heart regardless of social duty and fatally bent on mischief; and, therefore, it is implied from any deliberate or cruel act against another.

The rule is, that the implication of malice arises in every such case; and all the circumstances of accident, necessity, or infirmity, are to be satisfactorily established by the party charged, unless they arise out of the evidence and attending circumstances; if they do not, there is nothing to rebut the natural presumption of malice. This rule is founded on the plain and obvious principle, that a person must be presumed to intend to do that which he voluntarily and wilfully does in fact do; and that he must intend all the natural, probable, and usual consequences of his own act; and

[1] We have elsewhere called attention to the risks attending this simple procedure during pregnancy, and the necessity therefore of avoiding it at that time. (Boston Medical and Surgical Journal, October, 1859.) Instances are now within our knowledge where ladies have entrapped dentists, ignorant of their condition, into preparatory operations for false teeth, which were undoubtedly needed, and have thus very adroitly, from the shock to their systems, accomplished the special end they so much desired.

the having been coaxed into this act by an unhappy or wicked woman, is not admitted as excuse.

The standing in society of the accused, unless notoriously bad, should of course be allowed to weigh but little; the less the likelihood of the crime, the greater, from the example, influence, and previous education of the offender, its guilt.

If violent purging or vomiting have been resorted to without any apparent reason, or to a greater extent than is ordinarily prescribed or required; or if leeches have been applied to the thighs, to the number of a hundred or more, as instanced by Tardieu, or the like, — there is certainly ground for strong suspicion. And here it is that the criminal liability of careless or ignorant physicians becomes evident. In cases such as we have referred to, it would be very difficult for a successful defence to be offered, providing the pregnancy had been suspected by those not implicated, were the statutes on abortion properly drawn and enforced.

It has been ruled, and very justly, that attempts at the crime, though unsuccessful; or effective, and yet the ovum retained as a mole, hydatids, skeleton, mummy, or putrilage; and whether the woman be pregnant or not; and, if pregnant, whether the child be alive, dead, or abnormally developed or degenerated, — should be amenable as though fully consummated. We have seen the frequent difficulty in proving fœtal life: the attempt at its destruction shows the belief in its existence, and the intent. The proofs will here, of course, be of a different nature. The signs of delivery will be absent, and so also will be all evidence from the product of conception, unless the mother's death ensue; in which event, as in the other fatal cases we have considered, and on the principle just laid down, procedure might be had on the charge either of abortion or homicide; but it must not be forgotten, as we early pointed out, that immediate death from the shock may occur, and no lesion of any kind be found. The patient or parties interested are proved by the attempt to have supposed pregnancy existing, and to have behaved as though this were the fact.[1]

The age of the mother is not of consequence, save as relates to the question of her having passed or not passed the period of puberty, and her having reached or not reached the turn of life; nor is that of the fœtus, save as corresponding with the alleged period of pregnancy, and in case any doubt exist as to its own identity or that of the mother, and as bearing on the statement we have already attempted to prove, that criminal abortion is comparatively rare after the period of quickening, and, therefore, on the probability of intent. The number of the pregnancy is also wholly immaterial, different as are the causes alleged for its criminal induction, and equally liable in youth and age, as women seem to be, to accident or placental disease.[2] Whitehead and West are of opinion that abortion naturally

[1] We except here, of course, the very rare instances hereafter to be referred to, where abortion is necessitated at the hands of physicians to save the mother's life; and those other cases, more frequent but still rare, where the child having died in utero, and being retained in whole or in part, it becomes imperative to open up the uterus by dilating tents of sponge, or other material, for its removal; the mother's death often occurring from constitutional irritation, hemorrhage, or pyæmia, if this is not done.

[2] We have already stated, that, in some families, abortions are resorted to only with the earlier children, from a wish to defer the assumption of family cares; and, in other families, they are induced to only with the later children, the ordinary limit considered fashionable in the neighborhood, say, two or three, having been reached. In still others, it is systematically practised in every pregnancy, from motives of economy, the so-called prudence, or lust; seldom from fear of suffering, for women now generally know, that, by the use of anæsthetics, the pains, and we may say the dangers, of child-bed may be practically annulled. We are sorry to be compelled to add, to the shame of our profession, that, while it would be considered cruel for a physician to refuse a little camphor or peppermint or pennyroyal to one of our own sex with an ordinary belly-ache, very many are disinclined, or refuse, to relieve the unnecessary sufferings of women in child-bed, which in reality and ordinarily amount to an agony of which we men have probably no conception. Said Professor Simpson, of Edinburgh, at the last annual meeting of the British Medical Association, at Dublin, in August, 1867: "A man who should

resulting is most common after the sixth pregnancy,[1] but the point needs further investigation.

Among the proofs of intent must be included, as we have seen, the excuses offered by the accused or suspected party, and the means resorted to for consummation. These we now proceed to examine.

It will be evident that the plea of necessity can be made by none but a medical man. We shall show that the cases where abortion is legitimated by the rules of science are extremely few, and that for safety's sake their applicability should in no instance be allowed to rest upon a single opinion.[2] For all others beside the physician, there can be no allowable excuse, except, in the mother's case, insanity; which, however common in the true puerperal state, and often no doubt then showing itself by infanticide, has in early pregnancy, and to any extent, still to be observed.[3] Other pleas as offered by the mother, ignorance of pregnancy or of fœtal life, duress, impaired personal health or that of her family, accident, carelessness, fear of child-bed,

whip a poor sick woman with a cat-of-nine-tails, would be considered exceedingly cruel, and probably be punished by law for his cruelty. The act would merit some punishment; but the accoucheur who permits his patients to suffer the cruel pangs of child-birth, at this day, is guilty of a sin almost as heinous." Dr. Henry Bennet, the celebrated physician of London, expressed upon the same occasion an equally emphatic opinion. He stated, that, "if it were the law of nature that husbands should take turn about with their wives in bearing children, physicians would all at once become violent advocates of anæsthetics in child-bed." (Richmond Medical Journal, January, 1868, p. 859.)

1 Med. Times and Gazette, January, 1856, p. 611.

2 "This operation must not on any account be undertaken without the sanction, and in the presence, of another practitioner." Clay, Handbook of Obstetric Surgery, p. 13.

3 We must frankly avow, however, our belief that, during the whole period of pregnancy, women are not quite as accountable morally, however they may be legally, as when not in this condition; just as in the non-puerperal state, their minds are ordinarily somewhat differently affected at the menstrual periods than during the interval; a fact acknowledged by every woman who honestly confesses to her own sensations, and noticed by every observant medical practitioner, indeed by most married men.

malpractice on part of the attendant, we have already considered at sufficient length. It is sometimes effected in hatred of the husband or in jealousy, sometimes for concealment of shame; excuses of little more value than those of extravagance or fashion. Constitutional predisposition can hardly be asserted, unless the miscarriage have been preceded by others; very many ineffectual attempts are on record, although the existence of such predisposition was evident. It will often be alleged that the measures instituted were to prevent, instead of to effect, the miscarriage, and that this has resulted in consequence merely of an excess of good-will; the sophistry is generally apparent.

The means resorted to are for two purposes: on the one hand, to prepare the patient for the abortion and preliminarily to lessen her danger; or, to conceal the character of those, on the other hand, that really occasion it, and for this end used prior or subsequently to them. We may yet take occasion to consider these several agents in some detail; it remains only to remark that their use in any given case must be compared with what was then actually needed, or would have been required, had the abortion been justifiable and necessary.

Certain drugs, ergot and savin for instance, the class of so-called abortives popularly considered specific, are always suggestive of evil intent. They would not be used, were abortion necessary, by a well-informed practitioner, caring for the life of the parent or fœtus. The same is true, though of course to a more limited extent, of all over-drugging, over-manipulation, or over-exertion by a pregnant woman, by whomsoever advised or performed. In every instance, it is necessary to compare the cause alleged with the effects observed, and to judge of it from these. Where direct operative manœuvres are suspected or charged, the processes or instruments, the results, immediate and consecutive as well as remote, the period elapsing before their occurrence, must all be taken into careful consideration.

But, on the other hand, it is immaterial what was the agent, and whether or not it would produce abortion, if it was believed capable of this effect, and employed or administered with that intent. If the person charged knew that the woman was with child, and the probable effect of the agent administered, this is good presumptive evidence that the intent was to produce the miscarriage; and, where the effect of abortion is actually thus produced, it will materially aid the presumption of such intent.[1]

It was stated early in this inquiry, that a difference existed between the methods of investigation, as regards the examination of the fœtus, proper in abortion and infanticide. The reason of this has been pointed out by Tardieu.[2] In the latter case, the whole matter turning upon the questions whether the child, which must have been wholly born for the offence to have been committed, was born living or dead, and in which of these states it was injured, it becomes necessary to prove one or the other of the alternatives; but in abortion they are intrinsically of no importance whatever. The only points, then, to be decided are, Was the birth premature; and, if so, was it intentional; and, if so, was it absolutely essential, and to save either maternal or fœtal life? Except as bearing on these questions, therefore, it is of no consequence whether wounds were inflicted, whether the lungs had been inflated, whether the fœtus was viable, or even whether it was ever discovered.

In their place, however, these points are each important, but only as bearing on the main facts to be determined. In a case, for instance, like those related by Ollivier d'Angers, and Casper, of Berlin, where the fœtus, though very immature, lives several hours after its expulsion, this fact alone will preclude the idea of a slow and progressively acting cause, like most forms of abortive disease, and will point to some direct interference, by means suddenly terminating the pregnancy without injuring the fœtus.

[1] 1 Gabbett Crim. Law, 523.

[2] Loc. cit.

And so in other cases, especially of sudden maternal death, it is of importance to ascertain as nearly as possible the period at which the death of the fœtus took place. If the two were coincident, the deduction might be other than if the latter were proved to have preceded the former by several days. The differences observed between putrefaction and decomposition in utero and in the open air must not be lost sight of. In the former case, according to Orfila, Devergie and Martin, Moreau, P. Dubois, Danyau, Cazeaux, Tardieu, and our own experience, a uniform and characteristic reddish-brown hue obtains in proportion to the time of retention after death, varied perhaps by the action of the amniotic fluid;[1] the fœtus wrinkles, dries, and becomes mummified, unless in earliest pregnancy, when it generally resolves itself into a gelatinous mass.

If the cervix, the portion of the uterus most frequently wounded, is found punctured or lacerated, while the ovum is still retained, there is reason for suspicion; if the membranes are torn and extensively detached, while the cervix is but little dilated, such is increased; and it is made almost a certainty, if, with the latter condition, nothing remain of the ovum in the uterine cavity but lacerated fragments. Here the abortion would probably not merely have been intentionally induced, but by the direct introduction and agency of instruments.

Wounds of the fœtus are much rarer than those of the mother, and are usually simple pricks of the skin marked by blackish coagula or extravasations; which, if upon the skull and unless care be used, are liable to be simulated by clots casually adhering to the hair or scalp. If the wound be deeper, its course may be traced by dissection. Its situation varies; Devergie thinking it always on the back and buttocks, while Tardieu, with some warmth, would restrict its location to the top of the cranium. This difference is easily explained by variations in the time of pregnancy, and

[1] Chevalier and Devergie, Ann. d'Hyg., 1856, p. 157.

in consequence partly, as may also depend on its life or death, in the presentation of the child. The rarity of their occurrence, though denied by Taylor[1] and other medical jurists, might, however, be expected, and is readily accounted for; the instruments used by ignorant persons seldom entering the os, however severely wounding the cervix, and, where they do enter, usually only piercing the membranes; against which, except toward the end of pregnancy, in cases where there is a deficiency of liquor amnii, or in labor, the fœtus can hardly be said to forcibly press.

4. *The Identity of the Party Accused.*

Most of the points here involved having already been incidentally considered, we will not repeat them. The circumstances and history of the case, the relative correspondence of different testimony, the allegations of the accused, will all bear directly upon the question at issue.

In trials for abortion, of all others, the medical witness and the advocate should bear in mind their liability to error; the juror and the judge, the fact that innocent persons are at times wrongly accused, often by the true criminals themselves.

In defence, it must either be pleaded that the alleged abortion did not occur, that it was accidental or natural, that it was necessitated, or that it was induced by another than the individual charged.

The first of these pleas is seldom offered, except in the earliest months of pregnancy, and would be invalid if an attempt at the abortion could be proved. In default of this, however, where the ovum has been lost, or has passed unnoticed, the fact that the sanguineous effusion was hemorrhagic and attended with clots, would, in the absence of any uterine disease sufficient to account for this, be so far presumptive evidence; to be corroborated or not by the

[1] Med. Jurisp., GRIFFITH'S ed., p. 472, HARTSHORNE'S ed., p. 378.

history of the case. Moles and hydatids are now generally allowed to be mere transformations of the product of conception; their premature discharge, therefore, equally an abortion; their very occurrence, often the effect of attempts at the crime.

In answer to the second plea, the importance of several points must be borne in mind. It has been well put by Tardieu, that it is wrong to commence, as advised by most authorities on the subject, by enumerating all the natural and accidental causes liable to have produced the abortion. On the contrary, the signs and proofs of criminal violence should first be sought, and these compared with the allegations of witnesses and the possibility of a natural or accidental origin. The traces of falls, contusions, and wounds must be found, not believed on mere allegation; coincidences must be guarded against, equally with untruth.

We have already laid down rules here available: that the state of the fœtus often affords proof of the cause of its expulsion, this being slow and natural, and depending on disease and predisposition, or not; that in flagrant malpractice, the use of alleged specifics, or of measures likely to produce direct miscarriage, or otherwise absolutely counter-indicated by the general health and constitution of the patient, a contradiction exists to the plea offered, in itself strong presumptive evidence of criminal intent; and that, in certain cases, this evidence becomes positive, as where, for instance, a sponge found, or proved to have been inserted into the os uteri as a dilating tent, is alleged to have been intended as a mere pessary, and placed in the vagina.

If the accused be a physician, presumed, as he should be, to be acquainted with the great principles of practice, his only plea can be, where the means used were unjustifiable and proved such, and where the pregnancy was known to others, that he was ignorant of its existence. Liable as the profession are at any time to this charge, and easy as it is in almost every case, especially of instrumental procedure, for us to take such preliminary measures as would be likely to settle the question of the existence of pregnancy, or to request the presence of a witness to our act, it is unjust to ourselves and to each other to omit these precautions.

But if, on the other hand, the charge be utterly unfounded, it is probable, as I have already remarked, that contradictions in the testimony or the alleged facts could always be shown to exist, and the perjury thus exposed. It would be self-evident, were the accused proved to have been first consulted after the abortion had terminated, though not if it had only commenced.

CHAPTER V.

ITS PERPETRATORS.

It is interesting, and, at the same time, of judicial importance, to ascertain, so far as possible, the standing and character of the perpetrators of this crime.

In the first place, French statistics on the large scale show that the number of criminals, — principals, and accomplices, — in that country at least, is in large excess to the instances of the crime, there having been in 183 trials, from 1826 to 1853, not merely 417 parties accused, but 213 convicted; and that in 75 per cent of the prosecutions and convictions occurring, where the abortion is not induced by the mother herself, the offenders are women.[1] With us the same statement is, without doubt, equally true.

The part played by the mother, herself so often a victim, is almost always that of a principal; yet, as laws now stand, she can scarcely ever be reached. The cases where she is under duress, by threat of other personal violence from her husband or seducer, and thus compelled to submit to abortion, or where the act is performed by his direction but without her knowledge, are so rare, that, in a general statement, they may be assumed not to exist. If the mother does not herself induce the abortion, she seeks it, or aids it, or consents to it, and is, therefore, whether ever seeming justified or not, fully accountable as a principal. We have already seen the position these mothers hold in the community, high as well as low, rich as well as poor, intelligent and educated as well as ignorant, professedly religious as well as of easy belief, not single alone, but married.

[1] Tardieu, loc. cit., 1856, p. 124.

We turn now to their partners in guilt, more criminal than themselves; for, whatever excuse the latter may suppose themselves to possess, the former can have none.

The accomplices in criminal abortion are of several classes, distinguishable in some respects from each other, especially by the relative frequency with which their part is played. They are, of women, — 1. Friends and acquaintance; 2. Nurses; 3. Midwives and female physicians: and of men, — 4. Husbands; 5. Quacks and professed abortionists; 6. Druggists; 7. and worst of all, though fortunately extremely rare, physicians in regular standing.

1. In many cases, — such at least is judged by the writer from his own observation, — the abortion is not merely advised, but induced, by some female *friend*, especially by one who has herself undergone, in her own person, the crime; perhaps without appreciable evil result, — but this is not necessarily the case, for even where such result is present, and plainly in consequence, its connection with the true cause is frequently unsuspected or disbelieved.

It has been said that misery loves companionship: this is nowhere more manifest than in the histories of criminal abortion. In very many instances, from our own experience, has a lady of acknowledged respectability, who had herself suffered abortion, induced it upon several of her friends: thus perhaps endeavoring to persuade an uneasy conscience, that, by making an act common, it becomes right. Such ladies boast to each other of the impunity with which they have aborted, as they do of their expenditures, of their dress, of their success in society. There is a fashion in this, as in all other female customs, good and bad. The wretch whose account with the Almighty is heaviest with guilt, too often becomes a heroine. So true is the case, that the woman who dares at the present day publicly or privately to acknowledge it the holiest duty of her sex to bring forth living children, "that first, highest, and in earlier times almost universal lot," [1] is worthy, and should receive, the highest admiration and praise.

2. The ease with which an accomplice is procured, provided the idea originates with the victim herself, and is not suggested by another, is found among *nurses* to be greatly increased. We separate them as a class from midwives and female physicians, with whom, though in this country not generally acknowledged or thought identical, they not unfrequently aim to be confounded. They are usually, and rightly, thought more familiar with the laws of health and disease, than the generality of their sex; they are, if doing their duty in his sight, seen to be treated with respect by the physician; they are commonly of mature age, supposed discreet, wise, and to keep their own counsel; they have had opportunities of gaining the confidence of the mother; many of them have themselves borne families. They are therefore approached with less hesitation, and are not always found proof against an offered fee.

3. What we have said of nurses applies with increased pertinency to *female physicians* and *midwives*. These make it their claim, in rivalry of the male physician, that their schools and their practice are, like his, founded on those abroad, especially of Paris. Tardieu shows, in a total of 32 cases of criminal abortion occurring in that city and collected by himself, that in 21, no less than 66 per cent, or two-thirds of the whole number reported, the crime was perpetrated by midwives.[2] This class frequently cause abortion openly and without disguise. They claim a right to use instruments, and to decide on the necessity and consequent justifiability of any operation they may perform. Where they establish private hospitals, professedly for lying-in women or not, their chances, previously great, of committing this crime and infanticide with impunity, become more than doubled. It has been found necessary in France for

[1] A Woman's Thoughts about Women. By the author of "John Halifax, Gentleman." 1858, p. 14.

[2] Loc. cit.

the police to exercise rigid surveillance over these establishments. In one instance, occurring at Grenoble, it was proved that within three years there had happened in the house 31 still-births at the full time, or deaths just after birth, and that the abortions and miscarriages had been almost innumerable.[1] In another case, to conceal the evidence of these truly *corpora delicti*, and to evade the law against secret burials, the midwife had established a current account with an undertaker, who was accustomed to smuggle the fœtuses into his coffins, by the side of the corpses confided to him for burial. In still other cases, the victims are kept on hand, preserved in jars; private collections, vying in extent with those of legalized obstetric museums.

By these remarks we would not be supposed endeavoring to excite prejudice against female physicians and midwives as such, or advocating their suppression. We are now merely considering this crime of abortion, in relation to which they are peculiarly and unfortunately situated. At present, every thing favors their committing the crime: their relations to women at large, their immunities in practice, the profit of this trade, the difficulty, especially from the fact that they are women, of insuring their conviction. Let better laws be enforced, and let public opinion be enlightened concerning the guilt of abortion, and the influence for evil of this class of offenders will in great measure be done away with.[2]

[1] Loc. cit.

[2] The above remarks were written in 1859. Since that time we have made public and ample trial of the possibility of females becoming as competent as can men for the practice of physic; a question which involves also the propriety of their attempting to do so even were it possible. For three years we were attached as surgeon to a hospital mainly under the charge of such ladies, and for two years our assistant in private practice was a female physician. The experiment, as we have said, was long and honestly tried; and our conclusion, as expressed in our letter of resignation to the officers of the institution above referred to (Boston Med. and Surg. Journal, Sept. 1866), was to the following effect: that, granting that women in exceptional cases may have

Of male abortionists we have less to say. Their number is fewer abroad, bearing the proportion, as we have seen, of but one to every four; and their liability of being applied to or consulted is slight in comparison.

4. *Husbands*, though generally knowing to the offence of their wives, and often counselling it, probably but seldom attempt its commission themselves; yet instances of this do undoubtedly occur.[1] In but a sixteenth of the cases reported by Tardieu was any compulsory violence exerted over women by their husbands.

5, 6. *Professed abortionists* and *druggists* are accountable for the greater number of the cases of the crime attributable to men. The former class, though proportionally rare, yet abound in every city, and take all means of making themselves known. A knowledge of their alleged specifics, against the use of which, "at certain times," the public are "earnestly cautioned," &c., is brought home to all our women, no matter how purely minded, and despite every care to the contrary, through the medium of the daily press; few papers, however professedly respectable or religious, proving able to refuse the bribe.

all the courage, tact, ability, pecuniary means, education, and patience necessary to fit persons for and sustain them in the difficulties, cares, and responsibilities of professional life, they still are and must be subject to the periodical infirmity of their sex: which for the time, and in every case, however unattended by physical suffering, unfits them for any responsible effort of mind, and, in many cases, of body also. This is the true ground of objection, too often lost sight of. We have already referred to the mental influences of menstruation, and its effect upon individual responsibility; the condition being recognized and willingly acknowledged by those of the sex who have not some interested motive in denying it. It is not to women as physicians we would object, for they would often make most agreeable and charming attendants; but it is to their often infirmity, during which neither life nor limb submitted to them would be as safe as at other times. We could hardly allow to a female physician convicted of criminal abortion the plea that the act was committed during the temporary insanity of her menstruation; and yet at such times a woman is undoubtedly more prone than men to commit any unusual or outrageous act.

[1] We have referred to this matter in fitting terms in our book for the private perusal of men.

Druggists, as a class, are little more than the confessed agents of these villains. Even should they not directly recommend their nostrums, as, however, is frequently the case, they almost universally keep them on sale, labelled to catch the eye, and placarded on their walls. Like the publishers and vendors of obscene literature, they conceive they are not to blame for supplying a public demand, however much they themselves may have done toward its creation.

And in this connection we must again allude to the guilt of the public press, which has proved itself so constantly and so dangerously an accessory to the crime. It would be thought that in Massachusetts, for instance, a statute like the following might do something to check this license: —[1]

"Whoever knowingly advertises, prints, publishes, distributes, or circulates, or knowingly causes to be advertised, printed, published, distributed, or circulated, any pamphlet, printed paper, book, newspaper, notice, advertisement, or reference, containing words or language giving or conveying any notice, hint, or reference to any person, or to the name of any person, real or fictitious, from whom, or to any place, house, shop, or office, where, any poison, drug, mixture, preparation, medicine, or noxious thing, or any instrument or means whatever, or any advice, direction, information, or knowledge, may be obtained for the purpose of causing or procuring the miscarriage of any woman pregnant with child, shall be punished," &c.[2]

The above statute, however, such is the public sentiment on this point, is not enforced, or is daily evaded. The press, if it choose, may almost annihilate the crime: it now openly encourages it.

7. It has been often alleged, and oftener supposed, that *physicians in good standing* not unfrequently, and without

[1] Gen. Sts. of Mass. ch. 165, § 10.

[2] "By imprisonment in the State prison, or jail, not exceeding three years, or by fine not exceeding one thousand dollars."

lawful justification, induce criminal abortion. This statement, whatever exceptional cases may exist, is wickedly false. The pledge against abortion, to the observance of which Hippocrates compelled his followers by oath,[1] has ever been considered binding, even more strongly of late centuries. The crime is recognized as such in almost every code of medical ethics; its known commission has always been followed by ignominious expulsion from medical fellowships and fraternity. If this direct penalty be at any time escaped, it is only through lack of decisive proof; bare suspicion even of the crime insuring an actual sundering of all existing professional friendships and ties, — a loss that subsequent proof of innocence could hardly restore. Such is the unanimous feeling of the profession. To its credit be it said, that, with but a single exception,[2] — and this to his eternal disgrace, — its writers are all agreed, abstractly considering the subject, on the sanctity of fœtal life. The instances, where physicians in good standing are guilty of the crime, are of rare occurrence; the error that has prevailed on this point originating from the self-assumed titles of notorious quacks and knaves. But no condemnation can be too strong for the physician who has thus forgotten his honor; who has used, to destroy life, that sacred knowledge by which he was pledged to preserve it.

The criminal abuses likely to arise from the procurement of justifiable abortion by medical men are so numerous, their own liability to be thought by the public criminally careless of fœtal life, or sceptical concerning its existence, is so great, that the subject is worthy special consideration. This we shall now devote to it.

[1] Opera omnia. Ed. 1655, i., p. 643.

[2] Jörg, of Leipsic, who speaks of the human fœtus as "only a higher species of intestinal worm, not endowed with a human soul, nor entitled to human attributes."

CHAPTER VI.

ITS INNOCENT ABETTORS.

We have referred to an apparent disregard of fœtal life, obtaining in the medical profession, as a prominent cause of the prevalence of criminal abortion. We now proceed to show that the opinion is not unfounded.

Premature labor, or obstetric abortion, may be justifiably induced by the physician for one of two reasons, — either to save the life of the mother, or that of her child. In each case it must be, absolutely and only, to save a life.

Perfórmed for the child's sake, it is evident that the operation can be only available during the last three months of pregnancy; for then only can the fœtus with any degree of probability be considered viable. We grant that there are a few cases on record where, born during the sixth month and even in the fifth, the child has survived; but it is equally certain, despite the popular notion concerning the mortality of eighth-month children, that the later the operation can be safely delayed, the better the chance for the infant's life.

The rules for the induction of premature labor must, of course, vary for different cases. In this early stage of the inquiry, it is perhaps impossible to state them precisely, but they may still be approximately arrived at.

1. The operation, performed for the child's sake, is but seldom required; and in general,

2. Only after the commencement of the seventh month of pregnancy.

3. It must be clearly indicated; and

4. Must be delayed as long as is consistent with the child's safety.

5. Its means must be those which are most efficient, and safest for the child.

We have already stated, that the induction of abortion before the seventh month, undertaken for the child's sake, must be generally useless; and therefore, as attended with some degree of danger to the mother, generally unjustifiable. As the profession are nearly united on this point, its further discussion is here unnecessary.

We have asserted, that the cases where prematurely induced labor is required for the child are comparatively rare. We now add, that, while in some respects they are more frequent, in others they are less so than is generally supposed. To necessitate it, there must be disease or deformity on the part of the mother, or disease on the part of the fœtus or its appendages.

It is most frequently performed to avoid the alternative of craniotomy, or destruction of the child by evacuating the contents of its cranium; the necessity of which, unless extreme, can manifestly only be known with certainty, before the expiration of pregnancy, from the experience of past labors with the same patient. But here too much caution cannot be exercised; the rules of the books and of accepted authorities are not to be blindly followed.

Craniotomy at the full time is still too frequently performed; for, where it has been suggested by the character of a previous labor, children are often, or might be, born living: where it seems indicated by direct exploration, as ruled even by recent writers, children are sometimes, or might be, born living: where it was formerly thought absolutely essential, the progress of obstetric science has now rendered it often unnecessary.

It is proper that we consider these points, for they bear directly on the question at issue concerning criminal abortion.

It is known that the sex of children exercises an appreciable influence upon the result of labors at the full time, as regards the possibility of their passing alive, unaided or at all, through the pelvis, and as regards the length of the labor, which also progressively endangers the life of the mother and their own; the average female fœtus, in cases at all difficult, having the advantage over the male by its inferiority in size, especially important in the cranial diameters. It is unnecessary for us to do more than refer to the facts by which these assumptions are proved.[1] Where, therefore, craniotomy has been found necessary in a former labor, the child then being male, in another labor a female fœtus may often pass uninjured. However this argument may be lessened in value by the impossibility of previously ascertaining the sex, it is strengthened in the doctrine of chances, by the number of the labor and the sex of the former children; and by the fact that first labors are generally most difficult, whatever the sex of the child.

Furthermore, cases will suggest themselves to most practitioners of experience, in which, from difference in the character of the labor, or without apparent reason, children are born living at the full time, males of large size, and presenting by the vertex, where craniotomy had previously, perhaps repeatedly, been performed. An instance of this has occurred to the writer, where the patient had been advised to early abortions from alleged physical incapacity of ever bearing living children; he delivered her, without difficulty, of a large-sized and living boy, at the full time.

Again, it may happen, that, in labor at the full period, craniotomy may seem decidedly indicated and advisable, but for one reason or another may not be performed, and yet the child, unaided, be born living. The writer's experience prior to 1862, when he relinquished the practice of midwifery, furnished him with several illustrations of this class. One of these occurred in 1851, the patient having been his own, and Drs. Storer, sen., and Cabot, being in consultation; the other was seen at Edinburgh, in 1854,

[1] SIMPSON, Obst. Works, i., pp. 352, 404.

in the practice of a friend, Dr. Graham Weir. In both of the cases, permission was refused to operative procedures, the patients being Catholic, and the physicians unable conscientiously to pronounce the fœtus already dead, while the possibility of intra-uterine baptism was not recollected; in both instances the children were born living, and without instrumental aid.

In other cases, where, from deformity previously diagnosticated, craniotomy is pronounced necessary if the patient should go her full time, she may do so, the labor be unassisted, and the child yet escape with its life. We long since instanced a remarkable case for some time under our own charge at the Boston Lying-in Hospital, delivered by one of our colleagues, Dr. Dupee, and subsequently reported by Dr. Read.[1] The pelvis was here equably contracted, and to a great degree; but from some difference of opinion, partly as regarded the justifiability of premature labor as compared with craniotomy, the patient was allowed to go her full time. Both mother and child did well.

Finally, by turning, the use of the long forceps, and of anæsthesia, children are now constantly saved, where formerly craniotomy and their consequent destruction would have been absolutely indicated. These processes, with the introduction of each of which as an alternative a single name, that of Sir J. Y. Simpson, of Edinburgh, is imperishably connected, are now successfully employed by very many of the profession;[2] they have each of them saved to the writer the disagreeable necessity of fœtal destruction. Where, however, one life is thus preserved, there are still multitudes unnecessarily, and therefore unjustifiably, sacrificed.

[1] Boston Med. and Surg. Journal, January, 1857, p. 462.

[2] The immorality of craniotomy, where delivery can be effected by any other method, is gradually becoming acknowledged in Great Britain. A discussion on this subject, at the Obstetric Society of London, was reported in the Medical Times and Gazette for February, 1859; and there have been several since.

The comparative frequency of craniotomy in the different countries of Europe is in this connection worth noticing.

The operation was performed, in 1850–55, according to statistics we presented in 1859, in —

Germany	once in every			1944	labors
Paris	,,	,,	,,	1628	,,
France at large	,,	,,	,,	1200	,,
Vienna	,,	,,	,,	688	,,
England	,,	,,	,,	220	,,
Ireland formerly[1]	,,	,,	,,	128	,,
Ireland at present, Dublin Hospital, 1854[2]	,,	,,	,,	105.7	,,

The remarkable difference between the practice on the Continent and in England, so suggestive to us in this country, is undoubtedly owing to the fact, that, in Catholic States, a greater value is attached to the life of the child than "in Protestant States, as Britain, where the child is always sacrificed to save the mother."[3] The immense excess of embryotomy cases in Catholic Dublin furnishes no exception to this rule, drawn as they are from hospital practice under Protestant control.

"Whenever," writes Professor Elliot, of New York, "there exists a hope that the child may still be living, embryotomy must not be resorted to, unless other elective operative measures have failed, and perhaps have failed in more than one trial. Nor even then is embryotomy justifiable, unless the consultation are convinced that further delay must certainly preclude every chance of safety for the child, and very seriously endanger the maternal tissues, or life."[4]

So far proof by deduction. In many cases involving the question of craniotomy, that operation is not required; in some of them, not even the induction of premature labor.

Two classes of cases remain, each affording more direct

[1] CLAY, Obstetric Surgery, p. 68.

[2] SINCLAIR and JOHNSTON, Practical Midwifery, 1858. 130 cases of craniotomy in 13,748 labors.

[3] CLAY, loc. cit., p. 69.

[4] Obstetric Clinic, 1868, p. 314.

evidence ; those where craniotomy being absolutely indicated if the patient were allowed to go her full time, that operation is, and those where it is not, performed.

Craniotomy, being necessarily fatal to the fœtus, is indicated only to save the mother's life ; and it is to be avoided when any other alternative giving the fœtus a chance of life, and not more than equally hazardous to the mother, can be resorted to. Especially is this the case when it is compared with the induction of premature labor, attended as is the latter, despite a certain amount of danger of its own, with great probability of saving the child, and with decidedly lessened risk to the mother ; for craniotomy not merely requires the use of murderous instruments, dangerous to all tissues they may approach or be in contact with, but the operation is usually, though often very improperly, delayed till late in the labor, and therefore till the mother's chances of recovery have been proportionally lessened. Premature labor, on the other hand, though of course involving some risk to the child, is not necessarily fatal to it ; nor is it usually so, when properly performed. That there is a choice in this respect between the means employed, will hereafter be shown.

Craniotomy, when absolutely indicated at the close of pregnancy, must be for one of two reasons : that the fœtus cannot pass through the pelvis at the full time alive, though it may do so unmutilated, the operation being performed to save the mother the greater risks of protracted labor ; or that it cannot pass at the full time unmutilated, even when dead. We defer the consideration of another supposable instance, where the fœtus in the outset of its viability may pass, but not alive, for this pertains to the consideration of the mother's safety alone, no alternative availing for the child. In the other cases, if the necessity could be learned in season from the previous history of the patient or by pelvic exploration, labor should most certainly be prematurely induced, as affording some positive chance of life to the child, and as less dangerous to the mother. It were here worse than foolish, if not criminal, blindly to imitate nature, when, her course being obstructed, she would kill the child.

We have alluded for a double reason to cases, fortunately few, where, craniotomy and much more decidedly premature labor being indicated, the practitioner decides from the outset to perform neither, and to give his patient or her child no aid. Such conduct is as cruel and wicked as it is unprofessional; and, were not instances occasionally reported, its existence could hardly be believed. We acknowledge with Blundell the evils of meddlesome midwifery, but there are extremes to all things; certainly to the powers of nature and the limits of justifiable delay.

We are aware that we have referred to a reported case, which might in this connection be quoted against the opinion now expressed; but even by its exceptions do we prove the rule. Where chances are so greatly against both mother and child as in these cases if left unaided, it would be the office of the physician, were there no better procedure, by craniotomy to save the one;[1] but at the present day it is no less plainly his duty, where possible, to anticipate labor, and thus save both. We have elsewhere discussed this question at some length,[2] and can only repeat, as is indeed allowed by Churchill,[3] that this is no matter on which to select one's words; the deliberately sacrificing an unborn but still living child, in cases where statistics go to prove that the

1 The subject of justifiable craniotomy has been ably though controversially discussed by an anonymous writer (Dublin Review, April and October, 1858), by Dr. CHURCHILL (Dublin Quarterly Journal of Medical Science, August and November, of the same year), and by others. Care must be taken, lest in assenting to the decided and imperative necessity of the operation in certain cases, and by a natural professional sympathy, too great frequency is allowed to this most horrible and appalling of all the operations to which physicians can ever be called.

2 Review of CLAY's Obstetric Surgery; Boston Med. and Surg. Journal, November, 1856, p. 283.

3 Theory and Practice of Midwifery, p. 348.

adoption of another mode of delivery, nothing counter-indicating, would give that child a good chance of successful birth, is nothing short of *wilful murder*, no matter by what schools or by what eminent men it may be sanctioned, and it should be branded as such by the profession.

But, undertaken for the child's sake, not merely should premature lqɐor be resorted to for the purpose of preventing craniotomy, but often in cases of incurable disease, acute and chronic, of the mother, where it is evident that she must inevitably, or even probably, perish before the full period of pregnancy has been attained. Instances of such acute disease will readily suggest themselves. The question here is merely between the operation under consideration, the Cæsarean section, and doing nothing. The last, suppose the fœtus viable and to be still living, would in many instances be decidedly unprofessional and unjustifiable. Cæsarean section after the mother's death is comparatively unsuccessful; and, before it, is so much more severe, and in all probability so much more quickly fatal, that premature labor should be preferred, unless death be already close at hand.

Instances of chronic incurable disease necessitating the induction of premature labor may not so readily occur to the mind. The shock of an abortion being frequently greater to the maternal system than that of labor at the full time, it is evident that this rule cannot be universally applied. It cannot in every case of thoracic disease, of the heart, for example, unless its own peculiar symptoms become so aggravated from progressing pregnancy as to render probable earlier decease of the mother, the operation then being performed partly on her account; not so much to save her life as to delay a little her death. But there are other and extreme cases, as cancer of the lower segment of the uterus, or indeed of its fundus, which may have been diagnosticated previously to pregnancy by the use of expansible tents, where the mother would probably perish in labor at the full period, with most probably the loss of the child also. Here, by premature labor, the child may be saved, and the mother's life — greater expansion of the uterus and its more probable laceration being prevented — possibly prolonged.

So far complications on the part of the mother necessitating premature labor for the sake of the child. There are others equally imperative, afforded by itself. Excessive size of the fœtus in comparison with a normal pelvis, as rendered probable or evidenced by previous labors, is hardly of less importance in connection with craniotomy, than where the pelvis is distorted or contracted, and the fœtus of natural size ; but the operation in question, as compared with premature labor, we have already sufficiently discussed.

Diseases of the placenta, congestive, inflammatory, or degenerative, are no less an indication, where known to exist, for an early delivery. Their diagnosis may be difficult, but yet not wholly impossible. The occurrence of the same disease in past labors, and evident intra-uterine disturbance as discovered by auscultation or by unnaturally frequent and strong fœtal movements, are, taken together, frequently sufficient to establish the fact. The impropriety of allowing such cases to proceed unaided cannot be too strongly insisted upon. By early delivery, if in previous pregnancies the fœtus have perished after the period of viability, and in addition, by special medication of the parent, if its death had usually occurred before that time, many valuable lives might annually be saved.

Premature labor as resorted to on the mother's behalf alone, putting aside the cases we have incidentally considered, where the lives of both herself and her offspring are of necessity taken into account, includes also its induction in the earlier months of pregnancy before the fœtus is viable. It may be required by diagnosticated malformation or monstrosity of the fœtus, and by malformations on the part of the mother; by extreme pelvic contraction, congenital or from rickets or malacosteon, preventing the natural passage of a fœtus after viability, by tumors incapable of elevation or displacement, by contraction of the vagina. or by other severe obstetric complications, either recent or of long standing. Of this last class of causes, obstinate vomiting, puerperal convulsions, which are by no means confined to the full period of pregnancy, dropsies, irreducible displacements of the uterus, varix of the external labial vessels, sometimes fatal by laceration from tension, are all instances in point. With regard to each, the necessity of the abortion must be determined with the greatest caution, and resort be had to it, the child still living, with reluctance; especially should this be the case if the complication be supposed on the part of the fœtus, so important is it to avoid its sacrifice, if possible, and the semblance of disregarding its own important claims. It must not be forgotten that the vomiting of pregnancy has been discovered to originate in many instances from simple uterine irritation, the stomach itself being healthy; a fact that explains the frequent inefficacy of any remedial agents exhibited by the mouth. This is so important a matter, it has been so little understood, and so many lives are dependent upon the treatment resorted to, that it is well worthy close attention. We have elsewhere presented a short paper upon the subject.[1]

The rules for the operation of premature labor when performed for the mother are the same as when for the child, save that, if absolutely required, it may be resorted to at an earlier period. If the child must necessarily be lost, the labor should not be long delayed.

There are several subordinate questions arising in this connection, neither metaphysical nor merely casuistic, but practical, and, because bearing on the increase of criminal abortion, directly involving human life to an indefinite extent, and thus important to the medical jurist. One of them we shall now mention.

Let physical incapacity to the birth of a living or viable

[1] Detroit Review of Medicine and Pharmacy, November, 1867, p. 485.

child through the natural passages be supposed to exist on the part of the mother; that this has been proved by examination, or by the result of a former labor, induced or at the full time: to save the mother's life, early abortion is once brought on and the child destroyed, the woman and her husband being of course informed of the true state of the case. Is it right or justifiable again to destroy the fœtus, and as often as sexual lust may repeat impregnation? Or should the patient be left to the risks of a subsequent Cæsarean section, which would at least give the chance of life to her child?

We are aware on which side of this question lies at present the opinion and the practice of the mass of the profession; that Nægele[1] and others[2] have ruled it right always to destroy the fœtus when a refusal to undergo the Cæsarean operation shall have been formally expressed by the mother; and that reports of instances where early abortion has been repeated, even to nine times upon the same patient, are still unblushingly published by men of the standing of Lever and Oldham.[3]

But, on the other hand, in his admirable justification of craniotomy where absolutely necessitated, Churchill makes use of the following language, which, though offered in another connection, is none the less pertinent here: "It is the due appreciation of these relative responsibilities [regarding mother and child] in difficult cases, that distinguishes the wise and experienced accoucheur; he preserves a just counterpoise between them so long as it is possible to fulfil both, and recognizes the proper moment when one ceases. *One*, I say, not *either;* for I protest against the notion that *we choose which of the two lives we shall save;* a

1 De jure vitæ et necis quod competit medico in partu. Heidelberg, 1826.

2 "Where one only can by any possibility be preserved, the female herself may use her right of self-preservation and choose whether her own life or that of her child shall fall a sacrifice." GUY, Principles of Forensic Medicine, p. 145.

3 GUY'S Hospital Reports, 1856, p. 12.

notion as false in theory as it is in practice. *No man dare make such a choice*, for we have neither the necessary knowledge nor the right nor the authority to decide which is the more important life and best worth preserving."[1]

"My own opinion is that such a course [the repetition of abortion] ought not to be adopted, but that pregnancy should be allowed to proceed, without interruption, to the full period; and when labor declares itself, that the infant should invariably be extracted by the Cæsarean section,"[2] which, when performed in season, is by no means necessarily fatal to the mother, and may preserve life to the child.

Said Professor Simpson to the British Medical Association, in August, 1867, at Dublin, which has always been the headquarters of craniotomy, "If a woman with a deformed pelvis would go on putting herself in the way of becoming pregnant, she ought to be made to take the risks of the Cæsarean operation, rather than be encouraged in her course by sacrificing the life of her child."[3]

The question now so plainly put is one for the profession soberly to discuss and to answer.

We have already shown that, in many cases where instrumental delivery or the induction of premature labor is apparently requisite, the mother, if a Catholic, is sacrificed to the supposed impossibility of administering the rite of baptism to the child. We do not, with some, allow that the physician is here justified in deliberately and falsely asserting the child's death, where such has not taken place, but we have revived the suggestion of a method by which this great and fundamental obstacle may be overcome. We assert that the negligence too often shown by physicians in these cases, the custom of practically leaving the mother and her child to their fate when instrumental delivery shall have been refused upon religious grounds sincerely enter-

1 Dublin Quarterly Journal of Medical Science, August, 1856, p. 10.

2 Radford, British Record of Obst. Medicine, 1848, p. 84.

3 Richmond Medical Journal, January, 1868, p. 58.

tained,[1] is, however wide it may appear from the point, directly incentive to the increase of criminal abortion. Provided the question of necessity is determined, but one course in these cases should be pursued, and that, the performance of intra-uterine baptism.

The objections usually made to the induction of premature labor — namely, the uncertainty of all pelvic measurements and of the exact period of gestation, the greater liability to malpresentation, and, from the uninvoluted state of the cervix, to the evils of a lingering labor — lose much of their force when tested by our preceding remarks. If resorted to, the means of its induction are various; and, as regards their justifiability, they present a decided choice. We here omit the consideration of the methods indirect or of doubtful efficacy, as draughts, general or local baths or bleedings, forced exercise, fatigue, and voluntary falls or blows, so frequently resorted to by the uneducated, or used, in addition to other procedures, by the designing, to mask the reality: these will be subsequently considered; and we confine ourselves, in comparing the other and more direct methods, only to ascertaining that which is safest and most efficacious, for these points alone can decide their respective justifiability.

The direct and reliable means of inducing abortion, in the physician's possession, are only instrumental. Draughts of all kinds, whether purgative, emmenagogue, or so-called specific, — aloes, ergot, or savin; or energetic poisons, expelling the fœtus through a sudden and profound disturbance of the whole maternal system, as arsenic or cantharides, — are too unreliable, unscientific, or dangerous

[1] The rules of the Catholic Church upon this point have been already referred to. Suffice it to say, further, that while they enjoin the Cæsarean and vaginal sections in preference to craniotomy and in cases of extra-uterine fœtation, yet turning, the use of forceps, and the induction of premature labor, where such are indicated, are distinctly allowed by them; although this fact does not seem familiar to many clergymen of the church referred to. Barry, Medico-Christian Embryology, pp. 41, 44, 45, 60.

either to mother or child. The justifiable methods are confined to those acting directly on the uterus and its contents, by dilating the os or detaching the membranes.

They are, rejecting the local application of belladonna as utterly inert,—

1. Local or distant and sympathetic irritation by the hand; medicinal applications; electricity or galvanism; irritation of the mammæ; ice to the sacrum.

2. Puncture of the membranes, and evacuation of their fluid contents.

3. Dilatation of the os, and separation of the membranes from the uterine walls by expansible tents; as of sponge, sea-tangle, slippery elm, gentian root, &c.; the introduction of instruments; or the injection of fluids.

The first of these modes, in all of its applications, has generally proved extremely uncertain in effect. We think, however, that the measures referred to are in reality of greater importance than is generally supposed, and that the diversity of experience noticed in their use may be satisfactorily explained. We have already pointed out that it is at regular times during pregnancy, corresponding to the suppressed menstrual periods, that a woman is most likely to miscarry, in consequence of accident or disease. It is at just these times, that abortion or premature labor may most easily be intentionally induced. The measures under discussion are, all of them, efficacious in increasing the amount of the menstrual discharge, where this is deficient. They will be found as efficacious for the other indication, provided the suggestions now made are borne in mind and acted upon.

The second method, though that usually attempted, is of real avail only toward the close of pregnancy, and is even then decidedly inferior to the last of those proposed; at an earlier period, it is probably unjustifiable. In thirteen cases reported by Lever and Oldham,[1] where labor was pre-

[1] Guy's Hospital Reports, 1856, p. 4.

maturely induced by puncturing the membranes, only four of the children were born living, and in all these the presentation was by the vertex. It has been shown that malpositions are much more frequent in earlier than later pregnancy, and, from evident causes, the comparative absence and weakness of the fœtal movements which govern its position in utero, and the want of correspondence in form between itself and the containing organ. Of the nine cases reported where the fœtus was dead, five presented by the vertex, and were therefore probably alive at the commencement of labor, as after death, previous to labor, malposition very generally occurs, except there be deficiency of the liquor amnii or the pregnancy have advanced to near its close.

Again, it appears from the same statistics, which as offered for another purpose are the more to be depended upon, that in the successful cases, where the child was born living, the length of time after the operation, and before the occurrence of pains, almost doubled that in the unsuccessful cases, where the child was lost; the sum of the hours in the four successful cases exceeding the sum in the nine unsuccessful ones. That is to say, in the one class of cases time was allowed for a certain amount of dilatation of the os and cervix and for some degree of detachment of the membranes, an approach, however slight, to the characteristics of normal labor; and, in the other cases, the labor was brought on at once, without either of the above processes having commenced, and when both uterus and its contents were totally unprepared. Had the times, moreover, from the commencement of labor to its close, been given in the two classes of cases, it would probably have been found that the relative proportions were reversed; that the sum of the hours in the unsuccessful cases exceeded that in the successful cases, as would be in strict accordance with the results to the fœtus.

In premature labor, as in that at the full period, the bag

of waters is required to be preserved until it has fulfilled its purpose: on the one hand, of a fluid wedge; and, on the other, of protection to the child from violence till it has fairly entered the pelvic brim. Puncture is also attended with the danger of directly wounding the uterine tissues.

The last of the methods referred to, dilatation and detachment, combined to a certain extent as they must necessarily be, is in close imitation of the processes observed in natural labor, and is recommended alike by its safety to mother and child, its certainty, and the ease both to physician and patient with which it may be effected.[1]

From the above remarks, it is evident that the profession need to exercise great caution, lest they directly, though unintentionally, become the abettors of criminal abortion.

[1] For a full discussion of the respective merits of the several methods instanced above, see SIMPSON, loc. cit., i., p. 738.

Where expansible tents are used for the purpose of inducing premature labor, those of properly shaped sponge are undoubtedly the best. We have experimented largely with sea-tangle tents, and for several reasons have abandoned them. Those of slippery elm, first proposed by ourself to the Medico-chirurgical Society of Edinburgh, in 1855 (Association Med. Journal, London, May, 1855; Boston Med. and Surg. Journal, November, 1855), are better for other purposes, as for relieving the pains of dysmenorrhœa. The same is true of gentian root; the results of our experiments with which we published in 1855, but which has just been brought forward as new by WINCKEL, in 1867 (Deutsche Klinik); while we were both of us antedated by HOEBERL in 1834. Some years since we contrived an instrument, very similar to one proposed by SPENCER WELLS for dilatation of the female urethra, which, from its simple combination of the three principles involved, we prophesied would prove of material service in the induction of premature labor. We showed, moreover, that it possessed advantages over expansible tents for many cases of uterine disease where dilatation is necessary, either for diagnosis or treatment. A description of the instrument, and of its first application to obstetric practice, was published in the American Journal of the Medical Sciences for July, 1859. As so often proves the case in scientific discovery, it appeared however, that another writer, Dr. KEILLER, of Edinburgh, had conceived the idea at about the same time with ourself, and that our publications were almost simultaneous. The plan was subsequently adopted by an energetic and influential accoucheur of London: our instrument was slightly modified by him; and now, under the name of BARNES's dilator, it is universally acknowledged, and resorted to, as the best method of inducing premature labor throughout the world. For a full discussion of the question of priority in this matter, see Boston Med. and Surg. Journal, July, 1863.

But this liability is not confined to the instances already mentioned, where abortion has been intentionally induced. Nor is the matter in question one affecting merely the public health and morals, like prostitution or syphilization. It is a liability directly to increase the unjustifiable destruction of human life; and its existence cannot be too strongly impressed upon our minds, and guarded against.

So true is this, that two of the French obstetricians, Moreau and Bégin, have not hesitated to express their fears, and not on religious grounds alone; the latter, with Tardieu, giving it as his conviction, that every physician should make a legal declaration of the act to the public prosecutor, immediately on inducing premature labor, even if the period of viability has been reached by the fœtus. The subject has also been discussed by the French Academy of Medicine;[1] and in Great Britain it has been referred to by Radford, in whose opinion an enactment is necessary, "entirely prohibiting obstetric abortion (before the period of viability), as the door for evil purposes is already too open, and would be still more so, if it was legally decided that, where performed on supposed obstetric grounds, no inquiry should be made."[2]

Whenever an abortion is induced by a physician, even if accidentally, it is liable to be thought intentional by the patient and her friends, and consequently by the community, so far as it becomes aware of the fact. Instances of this are within the writer's knowledge.

Accidental abortions, caused by a physician, may be from two causes: error or insufficient care in diagnosis, or the absence of all likelihood of the existence of pregnancy. When cases are reported in apparent innoçence of fault, and by eminent practitioners, of the pregnant uterus having been tapped for ovarian dropsy; of craniotomy having been attempted upon an infant's fundament instead of its skull, and of the same operation in another instance undertaken upon

1 Bulletin de l'Académie, xvii. p. 364.

2 British Record, &c., p. 82.

the promontory of the mother's sacrum, it cannot be alleged, we care not by whom, that this caution is unnecessary or these fears unfounded. The writer will state a few cases of many that have happened under his own observation. He has several times known abortion to be accidentally occasioned by the use of sponge tents;[1] the patients being near the close of their menstrual lives, and neither themselves nor the physicians in attendance supposing that the contents of the enlarged uterus could be fœtal. In one of these cases, the woman had never before been pregnant; and in another, not for many years. He has more than once known the introduction of an intra-uterine pessary to be followed by abortion, and the same to occur from the use of the intra-uterine sound. In none of these cases was there any probability of the existence of pregnancy, save in the fact that the patients were married. He has known abortion to be produced by the application of lunar caustic to the os, in a case where, from the character of the operator, no suspicion could be entertained of the uterus having been more deeply tampered with. He has himself, in two cases reported by him to the Suffolk District Medical Society, in a somewhat similar manner, unintentionally induced miscarriage. In one of these cases, the woman had aborted but a short time before. To abate its apparent effects, a strong caustic was applied within the uterine cavity, the patient declaring that no intercourse had occurred since her previous mishap. The result was as already indicated. In the other instance, a lady supposed to be passing the grand climacteric, and who had had no children for many years, was operated upon for artificial perineum; she also, as well as her husband, alleged that coitus had not been indulged in for several months. Some ten days or a fortnight after the operation, she miscarried.

In cases like these, the practitioner would seem to render

[1] I have elsewhere discussed this subject; American Journal of the Medical Sciences, January, 1859.

himself liable to the charge of malpractice, even though, by the improbability of malicious intent, he escaped that of criminal abortion. In all instances where there exists the slightest suspicion or possibility even of pregnancy, the only rule for operative interference must be, unless circumstances imperatively prevent, to wait the few months or weeks necessary to establish the diagnosis, by the detection of the sounds of the fœtal heart. Justice to the profession and to the risk of error demand that where such precaution is not had, it should be replaced by a consultation, which would at once dispel any suspicion of carelessness or malpractice, and prevent a criminal charge.

All that we have said regarding surgical obstetrics applies as forcibly to its medicinal procedures. Though draughts and potions of every kind are, as we have remarked, of doubtful or indirect efficacy for inducing abortion, yet with some of them instances of its occurrence do at times result; more particularly, as we have said, at the times corresponding to the menstrual period.

In supposed obstructive amenorrhœa, unless of several months' standing, and in early pregnancy where established, the physician who does not intend it, must take care lest accidentally or carelessly, by purging, vomiting, or over-bleeding, he produce a miscarriage.

But there is still another point in this connection we must not pass over. We state it in the following inquiries, received from one of the most eminent practitioners of the Eastern States, and put to us in all sincerity: —

"Are there not cases where a physician would be justified in suggesting a course such as he would use in amenorrhœa, even where he might *suspect*, but not *know*, the existence of pregnancy? Suppose a mother of several children, which she has had in rapid succession, and the physician feels assured that health, and possibly life, will be endangered if another pregnancy occurs: would he be criminal if he were to use common means for amenorrhœa if the menses have been absent six weeks? Are the cases always so plain that a man can decide, and may he not balance a choice of evils?"

Covering, as these questions do, much of the ground already gone over, we may answer them at once and decidedly in the negative. They apply more especially to the early months of pregnancy, where it is always impossible to know its existence; and were direct or probable emmenagogues, or instrumental interference, to be here allowed, criminal abortion might be always induced before quickening, sanctioned and permitted by the rules of medicine. To justify abortion, life must certainly or very probably be endangered, not possibly merely, which is true in every pregnancy, and might be alleged at every trial for the crime.

Hufeland advised, as a "golden rule," always to suppose the existence of impregnation in such cases, and to act accordingly; that is, to temporize long enough for the fœtus, if present, to make its sign. "Thereby," he says, "the physician will avoid much mischief, and preserve his conscience as well as his reputation."[1]

The ideas on this subject held by my friend are without doubt widely entertained by the profession. This book will have served a good purpose, and have saved many fœtal lives, if it do no more than carry conviction of the error, and its likelihood to indefinitely extend the crime.

Again, it is undoubtedly the case, that in all cases of maternal death during pregnancy, where the fœtus has arrived at the period of viability, its immediate extraction by the Cæsarean section should be effected. We have already referred to this subject; and Kergaradec, who has well written upon it, lays down the maxim that the operation should always be performed, even in the fifth month of pregnancy.[2] In some cases, of placenta prævia for instance, where the

[1] Enchiridion Medicum, p. 510.

[2] Question d'Embryologie Médicale, etc., Revue de l'Amérique et de l'Ouest, 1846.

chances are always more or less against the child's life, success is less probable; but this in no wise invalidates the necessity of the operation. The writer has himself performed it in the complication instanced, and in vain; but he would none the more hesitate, on this account, to repeat it. There can be no reason against the procedure in any case, and by it the child may possibly be saved. In the words of an older writer, "Est inhumanum, post obitum matris, fœtui pereunti et suffocari parato manus auxiliares denegare, et sæpè viventem adhuc cum matre mortuâ eodem tumulo contegere et obruere. Idcirco jurisconsulti eum *necis* reum damnant, qui gravidam sepelierit non prius extracto fœtu."[1]

A question has been raised concerning the rights of relatives in preventing the physician from such discharge of his duty. It has been asserted that "the father has not only the natural right of his relationship, but legal power; for Dr. Lever recently mentioned that he had consulted Dr. Alfred Taylor to know whether he would be justified in performing Cæsarean section after the death of the mother, without the consent of the father, as it appeared unjustifiable homicide to allow the infant to die. Dr. Taylor gave his opinion that, in law, the infant belonged to the father,—the infant with the life thereof; and that if Dr. Lever touched it, even to rescue it from death, an action would lie against him."[2] We must, however, declare such doctrine to be false and pernicious. If signs of the child's life remain, no physician should hesitate endeavoring to preserve it, unless restrained by actual force. We reiterate our conviction that such neglect, or seeming neglect, of fœtal life is an actual wrong, both against the individual and against society.

Similar points in which physicians are directly interested,

[1] JOAN. RIOLAN., Anthropographia, lib. vi. cap. vii. p. 589.

[2] CHURCHILL, Dublin Quarterly Journal of Medical Science, August, 1858, p. 22.

as tending by their apparent disregard of fœtal life to render themselves innocent abettors of criminal abortion, are not uncommon. Such are, neglect of efforts to prevent miscarriage when threatening, or where it has become an established habit, for in many instances the woman can now be enabled to go her full time; and of attempts at resuscitating still-born children where there is the slightest chance of success, and success has now been rendered much more probable by the methods of Marshall Hall and Silvester; the performance of operations of any kind upon a pregnant women, even tooth-drawing,[1] that might be delayed; the careless or unnecessary use of ergot; the relying upon a single and unaided opinion, where not one life only, but two, may be endangered.[2]

Other instances might be adduced; but enough has already been said, to prove that the importance of the subject we are considering, and the responsibilities resting upon the profession regarding it, demand, as we have elsewhere suggested,[3] that physicians should possess, should acknowledge, and should govern themselves by, an *Obstetric Code*, — the necessity of which will be made even more manifest, as we proceed in our investigation of questions pertaining to Obstetric Jurisprudence. We have referred to some of its leading principles, but have done no more than faintly foreshadow them.

Distressing in the retrospect, inconvenient frequently in the present,[4] such a code would undoubtedly prove; but it

[1] A case in point has been reported by the writer; American Journal of the Medical Sciences, April, 1859. He has elsewhere referred to others.

[2] In the tenth of our contributions to Obstetric Jurisprudence, entitled The Abetment of Criminal Abortion by Medical Men, we have more fully discussed this subject. New-York Medical Journal, September, 1866, p. 422.

[3] Reports to the Suffolk District Medical Society of Massachusetts, 1857, and to the American Medical Association, 1859.

[4] "It would in my opinion," says Ramsbotham, referring to the nature of fœtal existence, "be much better not to endeavor to explain the secrets of nature, so deeply hidden." (Obst. Medicine and Surgery, p. 309.) This belief seems still, in practice, very widely entertained.

is demanded of the profession by the progress of our science, by humanity, morality, and religion. Were the facts in the case more generally known, and the existence and sanctity of fœtal life more universally appreciated, it would be also demanded by public opinion.

We have now seen that "the absurd enactments still remaining on the statute book, the careless indifference with which society views the crime, the reluctance with which means are adopted to prevent its occurrence, its increase, and its frequent induction by obstetricians, are all evils which loudly and imperatively call for the closest investigation."[1]

We have stated that the prevalence of criminal abortion is in great measure owing to a seeming neglect of fœtal life, on the part of medical practitioners, and that in other degree it is attributable to ignorance by the community of the actual character of the offence, — an ignorance of physiological facts and laws; and on both these points abundant proof has been afforded of the truth of our assertions.

We have also stated that medical men, in all obstetric matters, are the physical guardians of women and their offspring; a proposition that none can deny.

We have seen that unjustifiable abortion, alike as concerns the infant and society, is a crime second to none; that it abounds, and is frightfully on the increase; and that on medical grounds alone, mistaken and exploded, a misconception of the time at which man becomes a living being, the law fails to afford to infants and to society that protection which they have an absolute right to receive at its hands, and for the absence of which every individual who has, or can exert, any influence in the matter, is rendered so far responsible.

Under these circumstances, therefore, it becomes the medical profession to look to it, lest the *whole* guilt of this

[1] CLAY, Obstetric Retrospect, March, 1848, p. 44.

crime rest upon themselves. The point is so important a one, that we may be excused for a few more words upon it.

And, in the first place, it might be asserted with some truth, that such is indeed the case. For, on the one hand, it was from physicians, as is proved by early medical literature, that the mistaken notions, both of the law and of the people, regarding intra-uterine vitality, were derived; and on the other, the apathy and silence still existing on this subject among medical men, though thousands and hundreds of thousands of human lives are thus directly at stake, and are annually sacrificed, can only be explained on one of two suppositions,—either that we do not yet really believe in the existence of fœtal life, though professing to do so, or that we are too timid or slothful to affirm and defend it. By the one alternative, a gross lie seems proved; by the other, a degrading and strange inconsistency.

But, we believe, this apparent negligence proceeds only from ignorance of the real duty of the profession. It is our aim, while setting forth a deliberate and carefully prepared opinion upon this point, to inspire, if possible, in our fellow-practitioners throughout the land, somewhat of the holy enthusiasm sure, in a good cause, to succeed despite every obstacle, and an earnest, uncompromising hostility to this result of combined error and injustice, the permitted increase of criminal abortion.

Enough has already been said, to show that there is need of increased vigilance on the part of medical men, lest they themselves become innocent and unintentional abettors of the crime.[1] If, on the other hand, the community were made to understand and to feel that marriage, where the parties shrink from its highest responsibilities, is nothing less than legalized prostitution, many would shrink from

[1] In this connection, we cannot too strongly deprecate a practice that has soberly been proposed; namely, the detection of the early existence of pregnancy by the administration of ergot. (Boston Med. and Surg. Journal, April, 1859, p. 197.) The use of ergot for this purpose, in however small a dose, would seem utterly unjustifiable.

their present public confession of cowardly, selfish, and sinful lust. If they were taught by the speech, and daily practice of their medical attendants, that a value attaches to the unborn child, hardly increased by the accident of its birth, they also would be persuaded or compelled to a similar belief in its sanctity, and to a commensurate respect.

But it has been asked, Is our silence wrong? Is there not danger otherwise of increasing the crime? These are the questions not of wisdom, or prudence, or philanthropy, but of an arrant pusillanimity. Vice and crime, if kept concealed, but grow apace. They should be stripped of such protection, and their apologists, thereby their accomplices, condemned. Answers, however, are ready at hand to the questions proposed.

"It is one of the great desiderata of registration, that more particularity should be observed, in collecting facts relating to the subject of the still-born."[1]

"Has it been sought," society demands of the profession, "to account for the peculiarities relating to the still-born, and to combat the causes which, in certain circumstances, swell their number in so deplorable a manner?"[2]

"An honest and fearless expression of these causes and circumstances, on the part of medical men, would bring to light an amount of knowledge, that might be useful in checking this horrible and increasing waste of life."[3]

"Such an exercise of his knowledge, experience, and true moral courage, is not only the province, but the conscientious duty, of the physician."[4]

"It should be constantly borne in mind, that there is here a high and stern morality, that should stimulate the medical profession in the exercise of their utmost effort and

[1] Fifteenth Massachusetts Registration Report, 1857, p. 199.

[2] QUETELET, Theory of Probabilities, p. 234.

[3] New-York Medical Gazette, editorial; London Medical Times and Gazette, 1850, p. 487.

[4] Boston Medical and Surgical Journal, editorial, 1855, p. 411.

ingenuity, with the view to master and disclose the secrets of these villanous practices; the more villanous, because they are very generally conceived in fraud, practised in deception upon innocent and unsuspecting victims, and result the most commonly in the destruction of two lives at once."[1]

"For ourselves, we have no fear that the truth in reference to the crime of procuring abortion would do aught but good. It would appear that sheer ignorance in many honest people is the spring of the horrible intra-uterine murder which exists among us: why not, then, enlighten this ignorance? It would be far more effectually done by some bold and manly appeal than by the scattered influence of honorable practitioners alone. Will not the mischief, by and by, be all the more deadly for delaying exposure and attempting relief?

"Whatever estimate may attach to our opinion, we believe that not only ought these things not so to be, but that the public should know it from good authority."[2]

"This is a topic which ought to be regarded of the highest interest to the profession and the public."[3]

"It is by far the most important subject before the profession, and, in its medical as well as moral bearings, appeals alike to our patriotism and humanity."[4]

"We think the public have very erroneous ideas of the turpitude of this crime; and we deem it our duty, as conservators both of the public health and morals, to set it in a correct light before them."[5]

"The question of criminal abortion is doubtless one of extreme difficulty; it is not, however, beyond the reach of the enlightened prudence and the firm will of the authorities. It is a subject of such vital import to society in gen-

1 Dean, Medical Jurisprudence, p. 139.

2 Boston Medical and Surgical Journal, editorial, Dec. 13, 1855.

3 American Medical Gazette, editorial, July, 1857, p. 390.

4 Ibid. April 1859, p. 289.

5 Maine Medical and Surgical Reporter, editorial, June, 1858, p. 39.

eral, that we feel convinced it cannot but awaken the anxious thought of the persons who, from their position, are intrusted with the application of the laws, and the control of public morals."[1]

Whoever shall succeed in fixing upon it the attention it deserves, "has taken a stand in this matter alike creditable to his head and his heart; and we feel that he will receive the hearty thanks of every true physician."[2]

"The increasing prevalence of infanticide," which is but rare compared with criminal abortion, "its dangerous moral influence, the apathy with which so many regard its spread, and the very considerable difficulty in obtaining conviction, call loudly for reform. The question is one of national importance."[3]

"With this view of the case before us, I suggest it as our imperative duty, to direct the attention of legislators to the importance of enacting a statute in conformity thereto."[4]

Such are the confessions, independently given, of high-minded and honorable medical men. No more can be added: no less would have been true.

It must be granted, then, that a bold and manly utterance of the truth, combining, as this must, contradiction of the error, and denouncement of the crime, should be made by the members of the profession on every occasion. By this course, it is plain that a healthier moral tone would be made to prevail in the community, the crime would become of rarer occurrence, and the laws, such as they are, would be more faithfully attempted to be enforced.

[1] Deville, Researches on the proportion of still-born children compared with the mortality of the City of Paris during the thirteen years, 1846–58. Memoirs of the French Academy, 1859.

[2] New-Hampshire Journal of Medicine, editorial, July, 1857, p. 216.

[3] London Lancet, editorial, July, 1858, p. 66.

[4] Tatum, Virginia Med. Journal, June, 1856, p. 457.

It will be noticed that I do not quote opinions of a later date than the first edition of this book. Since its publication, a host of commendatory notices have proved the wisdom of the step then taken.

But it has been shown that the laws on the subject of criminal abortion are radically imperfect and defective, and that this is attributable wholly to a medical cause. We assert, therefore, that not only is it the duty of the profession as individual components of society, but more especially as medical men, to see them amended, and to leave no means untried, no effort unmade, for the attainment of this end.

"Physicians alone," says Hodge, in his Introductory Address, "can rectify public opinion; they alone can present the subject in such a manner, that legislators can exercise their powers aright in the preparation of suitable laws; that moralists and theologians can be furnished with facts to enforce the truth upon the moral sense of the community, so that not only may the crime of infanticide be abolished, but criminal abortion properly reprehended, and that women in every rank and condition of life may be made sensible of the value of the fœtus, and of the high responsibility which rests upon its parents."[1]

It has been stated, indeed publicly avowed by a medical body,[2] that when a physician "shall become cognizant of any attempt unlawfully to procure abortion, either by persons in the profession or out of it, it shall be his duty immediately to lodge information with some proper legal officer, to the end that such information may lead to the exposure and conviction of the offender."

This doctrine is doubtless true to a great extent; but it cannot be applied to the confidential disclosures of patients themselves, which no man has a right to reveal, unless constrained by the direct command of the court, at which, it has been ruled, even professional secrets must be divulged.[3]

[1] Loc. cit. p. 19.

[2] The Councillors of the Massachusetts Medical Society. Proceedings of the Society, 1858, p. 77.

[3] Phillips on Evidence, i., p. 135; Ryan, Medical Jurisprudence, p. 193; Storer, sen., Introductory Address, 1855, p. 10; Simpson, Physicians and Physic, p. 31.

It follows, from the evidence we have now adduced, that, if it be the duty of the profession to urge upon individuals the truth regarding this crime, it is equally their duty to urge it upon the law, by whose doctrines the people are bound; and upon that people, the community, by whose action the laws are made.

And this should be done by us, if we would succeed in suppressing the crime, — not by separate action alone, but conjointly as the profession, grandly representing its highest claim, — the saving of human life.

Every step toward this end should be hailed with enthusiasm. The too halting action of the State Society of Massachusetts, directly resulting from professional agitation of the subject, yet deserves praise and imitation; the body referred to having passed a series of resolutions to the following effect: "That the Fellows of the Massachusetts Medical Society regard with disapprobation and abhorrence all attempts to procure or promote abortion, except in cases where it may be necessary for the preservation of the mother's life; and that no person convicted of such attempt can, consistently with its by-laws, any longer remain a fellow of the society."[1]

But the mere passage of resolutions in disapproval of this horrible and so rapidly increasing crime is not sufficient to effect its abatement. Something more has been wanted than the testimony of record books, the pointless vote of a board of councillors. We foretold that there must come a hearty, earnest, and unanimous voice from the mass of the profession, an assertion that criminal abortion, or at least its permitted commission, ought no longer to exist. As years have passed, this cry is beginning to make itself heard.

Too much zeal cannot be shown by physicians in relieving themselves from the weight of responsibility they may have incurred by innocently causing the increased destruc-

[1] Proceedings of the Society, 1858.

tion of human life. Let it not be supposed by the public that there is among us, either in theory or practice, any disregard of the unborn child. If such impression have already obtained, from our own negligence, the falsehoods of irregular practitioners, or otherwise, it should at once be removed. Fœtal life ever is, and ever has been, held sacred by all respectable physicians; and whenever criminal abortion has been known to have been advised, perpetrated, or abetted by one claiming our honorable name, he has invariably and at once lost all professional standing.

We have seen that it is no trifling matter, this awful waste of human life. It is a subject that demands the best efforts of the whole profession as a body and as men. The crime, no longer practised in secret, must be met boldly; and, met with unanimity, it will be met successfully.

But whether these efforts are to be at once decisive or not, whether they are to be received with the gratitude of the community or its disfavor, is no concern of ours. Our duty is very plain: it is to stand, irrespective of personal consequences, in the breach fast making in the public morality, decency, and conscience, and, to the best of our strength, to defend them.

It might be — it very likely would be — for our immediate pecuniary interest as a profession, to preserve silence; for we have shown that abortions, of all causes, tend to break down and ruin the health of the community at large. But to harbor this thought, even for a moment, were dishonorable. "I will never set politics against ethics," said Bacon; "for true ethics are but as a handmaid to divinity and religion."

We must take this decided stand, — there is no choice; else we are recreant to the high trust we have assumed, and to ourselves. Whether the suppression of abortion be effected or no, one thing is certain, our own hands will have been cleansed of this sea of blood. We shall have declared our abhorrence and our innocence of the crime.

Longer silence and waiting by the profession would be criminal. If these wretched women, these married, lawful mothers, — ay! and these Christian husbands, — are thus murdering their children by thousands, through ignorance, they must be taught the truth; but if — as there is reason to believe is too often the case — they have been influenced to do so by fashion, extravagance of living, or lust, no language of condemnation can be too strong.

Let us, then, meet the issue earnestly and boldly. Silence and patient expectance have been fairly tried: the disease is not self-limited: the evil, instead of working its own cure, has assumed a gigantic, an awful growth.

Abstract discussions of this matter, by ourselves, and within the closed doors of our several societies, no longer avail. We are all agreed upon the guilt of abortion: we ever have been. Our prayers for its suppression have not been answered, for they have hitherto been offered with inactive hand.

We should, as a profession, openly and with one accord appeal to the community in words of earnest warning; setting forth the deplorable consequences of criminal abortion, the actual and independent existence, from the moment of conception, of fœtal life. And, that the effort should not be one of words merely, we long since advised that medical men, as a profession, should recommend to the legislative bodies of the land the revision and subsequent enforcement of all laws, statutory or otherwise, pertaining to this crime, that the present slaughter of the innocents may, to some extent at least, be made to cease. For it is "a thing deserving all hate and detestation, that a man in his very originall, whiles he is framed, whiles he is enlived, should be put to death under the very hands and in the shop of nature."[1]

In accordance with this opinion, a committee, consisting of Drs. Blatchford, of New York; Hodge, of Pennsylvania; Pope, of Missouri; Barton, of South Carolina; Lopez, of

[1] Man Transformed. Oxford, 1653.

Alabama; Semmes, of the District of Columbia; Brisbane, of Wisconsin; and the writer, — was appointed by the National Medical Association, at its meeting at Nashville, in 1857, to report upon criminal abortion, with a view to its general suppression. The report of this committee, brief, but in strict accordance with the views that we have expressed, was made to the Association, at its session held at Louisville, in May of the ensuing year. The report was accepted, and the resolutions appended to it[1] were unanimously adopted.

In behalf of the committee, of whom he had the honor to be chairman, the writer cannot close this portion of his labors without thanking the physicians of the land, represented as they are by the Association, for their hearty and noble response to the appeal that had been made them. He would express, were it possible, the gratitude not of individuals, but society; for by this act the profession was again true to "its mighty and responsible office of shutting the great gates of human death."

We proceed to the other relations of criminal abortion, more especially to those immediately pertaining to the claims and course of justice.

1 "*Resolved*, That while physicians have long been united in condemning the procuring of abortion, at every period of gestation, except as necessary for preserving the life of either mother or child, it has become the duty of this Association, in view of the prevalence and increasing frequency of the crime, publicly to enter an earnest and solemn protest against such unwarrantable destruction of human life.

"*Resolved*, That in pursuance of the grand and noble calling we profess, — the saving of human life, — and of the sacred responsibilities thereby devolving upon us, the Association present this subject to the attention of the several legislative assemblies of the Union, with the prayer that the laws by which the crime of abortion is attempted to be controlled may be revised, and that such other action may be taken in the premises as they in their wisdom may deem necessary.

"*Resolved*, That the Association request the zealous co-operation of the various State medical societies in pressing this subject upon the legislatures of their respective States, and that the president and secretaries of the Association are hereby authorized to carry out, by memorial, these resolutions." (Transactions of the American Medical Association, 1859, vol. xii. p. 75.)

CHAPTER VII.

ITS OBSTACLES TO CONVICTION.

We have already seen that there are special, though, it is to be hoped, not wholly insurmountable, causes for the existing prevalence of abortion. It now becomes our duty to consider some of these reasons in detail, in so far as they relate to and obstruct the course of justice.

It would seem, from what has been previously said, that little doubt could be entertained of the inefficacy of our present statutes against abortion. There are few of the States whose laws on this point are so wisely and completely drawn as in Massachusetts; yet, as they there stand, they cannot, as such, be enforced. In that Commonwealth, according to the reports of the attorney-general, during the eight years from 1849 to 1857, omitting 1853, — as there seems to have been no report rendered for that year, — there were, as we have seen, 32 trials for abortion, and not a single conviction!

A committee of the State Medical Society of Massachusetts, to whom the propriety of a professional appeal to the legislature for more protective statutes had been referred by the District Society of Boston, having reported against such action, on the ground "that the laws of the Commonwealth are already sufficiently stringent, provided that they are executed,"[1] — it becomes the more necessary for us to

[1] Medical Communications of the Mass. Med. Soc. 1858, p. 77.

The writer, having been a member of this committee, again enters, as he has long since done by letter to the councillors of the Society, his earnest protest against the plainly erroneous opinion avowed in that report, which was presented and accepted during his absence from the State. He has taken occasion elsewhere to express himself even more plainly upon the

strike at the root of the whole matter, and to show, if possible, why conviction, unless in case of the death of the mother, cannot at present be obtained.

subject. A portion of those comments will here bear repeating, inasmuch as he intends, *Deo volente*, to see this matter righted. I have shown, that by any apparent disregard of the existence or sanctity of fœtal life, however evinced, we in reality increase its disregard by the community. If a physician appear to consider an unborn child of little or no account, why should not his patients also? I have also referred to this same unintentional abetment of abortion by medical men, in the prize essay of the American Medical Association. (Transactions of the American Medical Association, 1865, vol. xvi., p. 709.)

"Few will doubt that my opportunities have been good for observation in this matter. The decided opinions that I have avowed, met as they were at first by so free expression of scepticism and indeed of denial, could but awaken a corresponding degree of interest in minds alive to the importance of the subject; and my repeated consultation, personally or by letter, concerning abortion, by many of the leading practitioners of this country, may perhaps give a weight to the remarks I may now make, that formerly might have seemed presumptuous for me to claim.

"It will be recollected, that in 1859, by order of the American Medical Association, a memorial was presented in its name to 'the several Legislative Assemblies of the Union, with the prayer, that the laws by which the crime of abortion is attempted to be controlled may be revised, and that such other action may be taken in the premises as they in their wisdom may deem necessary;' and that the association also requested, by formal memorial, the zealous co-operation of the various State Medical Societies in impressing this subject upon the legislatures of their respective States (vol. xii., p. 75).

"This action was based upon a long, careful, and very thorough examination of the whole subject, by a competent committee, who were unanimously of the opinion that the action desired was necessary.

"A similar conclusion had previously been reached by a committee appointed by the Suffolk District Society, of Boston, in 1857, consisting of Drs. Bowditch, Calvin Ellis, and myself; and yet, in the face of the fact that in this Commonwealth, for some eight years, there were thirty-two trials for abortion, and not a single conviction, the Councillors of the State Medical Society of Massachusetts, to whom the propriety of a professional appeal to the legislature for more protective statutes had been referred, decided, that 'the laws of the Commonwealth are already sufficiently stringent, provided they are executed.' (Medical Communications of the Massachusetts Medical Society, 1858.)

"It is not, however, the stringency of a statute, — so far as by this is meant the severity of its punishments, — but the certainty of their infliction, that is efficient to check a crime. By the laws of Massachusetts, the crime of abortion is considered as mainly against the person of the mother. In the case

It has been thought, even publicly argued, that in the fact that statutes against abortion are almost everywhere not only not enforced, but not attempted to be enforced, there is

of her death, already sufficiently provided for at common law, convictions can indeed be effected, though with great difficulty, under the statute. If she lives, the crime practically goes unpunished. It is true, that a few convictions have been obtained with us since 1863, but only by great effort, and probably in consequence mainly of the attention we have called to the subject.

"I have elsewhere directed notice to this fact, and to its explanation, and to the causes of the general demoralization as regards child-bearing.

"'There are three of these causes, however,' say the committee of the American Medical Association, and they are the most important with which the medical profession have especially to do.

"'The first of these causes is a wide-spread popular ignorance of the true character of the crime,—a belief, even among mothers themselves, that the fœtus is not alive till after the period of quickening.

"'The second of the agents alluded to is the fact, that the profession themselves are frequently supposed careless of fœtal life; not that its respectable members are ever knowingly and intentionally accessory to the unjustifiable commission of abortion, but that they are thought at times to omit precautions or measures that might prevent the occurrence of so unfortunate an event.

"'The third reason of the frightful extent of this crime is found in the grave defects of our laws, both common and statute, as regards the independent and actual existence of the child before birth, as a living being. These errors, which are sufficient in most instances to prevent conviction, are based, and only based, upon mistaken and exploded medical dogmas. With strange inconsistency, the law fully acknowledges the fœtus in utero and its inherent rights for civil purposes; while personally, and as criminally affected, it fails to recognize it, and to its life as yet denies all protection.' (Report on Criminal Abortion, p. 3.)

"To the action of the Councillors of the Massachusetts Medical Society, in 1858, based as it was upon the report of the committee appointed by the State Society at large, consisting of Drs. Foster Hooper, Jacob Bigelow, John Ware, J. C. Dalton, Ebenezer Hunt, Charles Gordon, and myself, drawn up and rendered during my necessary absence from this part of the country, and without my being in any way conferred with, I entered, by letter to the councillors, my earnest protest. This protest, so far as can be judged by the published proceedings of the councillors, seems never to have been acted upon.

"I should have long since brought the matter before the profession at large, had I not been prevented by ill health. That cause no longer exists; and after the lapse of eight years, during which, the subject has never by me been lost sight of, I am but the more confirmed in the opinion that a grave error was committed by my colleagues. By the vote of the councillors, there was furnished additional ground for the third of the causes mentioned

afforded strong evidence of the existence of an ultimate and absolute impossibility of thus meeting the crime. The idea, though a fallacious one, is yet attributable to an important and evident cause.

That the prevalence of abortion is in great measure owing to ignorance of guilt, on the part of the community at large, we have shown. We now assert that its futile prohibition by the law, its toleration, are plainly in consequence of similar ignorance on the part of legislators, and of officers of justice.

Our communities form their own laws; and, therefore, as was pointed out at the commencement of our remarks, these must necessarily bear the stamp of public opinion; while the officers by whom they are to be enforced, — juror, attorney, judge, — looking to the only source possible for their enlightenment on this subject, — to medical men, — had, until 1858, found but few bold and honest statements,[1] and these unindorsed by the mass of the profession; or, in the total silence, a practical sanction of the popular belief. This is no exaggeration; the assertion is fully borne out by facts. Need we wonder, then, that the laws are not enforced, that indeed their enforcement is not attempted? But this first and great cause, it is apparent, is by no means an essential one.

We need add nothing to what we have already said of those obstacles to conviction arising from circumstances

above, by which the profession become directly accountable for the increased frequency of the crime.

"The resolutions adopted by the councillors upon the occasion referred to may have been supposed by some to fully cover the required ground. They are, however, speciously framed: they in reality amount to nothing, begging the vital question, as they completely do; and, as one of the committee by whom they were offered, I again repudiate them." (New-York Med. Journal, Sept. 1866, p. 427.)

[1] In this connection, honorable mention is due Drs. TATUM and JOYNES, of Virginia, for their papers on "The Attributes of the Impregnated Germ," and "Some of the Legal Relations of the Fœtus in Utero." (Virginia Medical Journal, 1856.)

common in greater or less degree to other crimes, — the difficulties of detection and of obtaining proof, however great these are allowed to be; but we shall soon proceed to consider the laws themselves by which in this country the crime of abortion is attempted or is expected to be suppressed.

If our previous assumptions of the actual character of criminal abortion be granted, — and we believe that they have been proved to a demonstration, — it will be found from their application that the common law, both in theory and in practice, is insufficient to control the crime; that, in many States of this Union, the statutory laws do not recognize its true nature; that they draw unwarrantable distinctions of guilt; that they are not sufficiently comprehensive, directly allowing many criminals to escape, permitting unconsummated attempts at abortion, and improperly discriminating between the measures employed; that they require proofs often unnecessary or impossible to afford; that they neglect to establish a standard of justification, and thereby sanction many clear instances of the crime; that, by a system of punishments wholly incommensurate with those inflicted for all other offences whatsoever, they thus encourage instead of preventing its increase; and that in many respects they are at variance, not merely with equity and abstract justice, but with the fundamental principles of law itself.

"It is to be hoped," has forcibly been written, "that the period is not far remote, when laws so cruel in their effects, so inconsistent with the progress of knowledge and civilization, and so revolting to the feelings and claims of humanity, will be swept from our statutes."[1]

In a similar trust, it behooves us to consider whether, and in what manner, the difficulties in the way of generally suppressing the crime of abortion can be overcome.

[1] Lee, Note to Guy's Principles of Forensic Medicine, p. 134.

To the question, whether it can be all controlled by law, we do not hesitate to give an unqualified answer in the affirmative. The fact, that criminal abortion is not controlled by law anywhere, cannot be entertained as a valid argument to the contrary of this assertion; for it is equally the fact, as we shall see, that laws against abortion do not as yet exist which are in all respects just, sufficient, and not to be evaded.

It is evident, that, in aiming to suppress this crime, the law should provide not merely for its punishment, but indirectly as well as directly, and so far as possible, for its prevention. The punishment of a crime cannot be just, if the laws have not endeavored to prevent that crime by the best means which times and circumstances would allow;[1] and this is to be accomplished by a twofold process: by rendering, on the one hand, its detection more probable, and, on the other, its punishment more certain.

As indirect though important measures for the former of these ends, we have already mentioned laws for registration,[2] and against concealment of births and secret burials. As a single proof of their possible influence in this respect, out of many that might be adduced, we instance the fact, that, in Paris, the number of premature fœtuses deposited at the Morgue during the nine years from 1846 to 1854, inclusive, was found to exceed by more than two-thirds that of the full decade just preceding, from 1836 to 1845.[3] To

[1] Beccaria, Crimes and Punishments, 104.

[2] "An efficient and practical remedy for the prevention of this crime would be a law requiring the causes of death to be certified by the physician in attendance, or, where there has been no physician, by one called in for the purpose. In this way, the cause of death, both in infants and mothers, could be traced to attempts to procure abortion. In three cases which occurred in Boston, in 1855, the death was reported by friends to be owing to natural causes, and in each it was subsequently ascertained that the patient died in consequence of injuries received in procuring abortion. It is probable that such cases are by no means rare; and, if the cause of death were known, an immediate investigation might lead to the detection of the guilty party." (Boston Medical and Surgical Journal, Dec. 1857, p. 365.)

[3] Register of the Morgue.

render this difference more apparent, we have compiled the following table: —

Age of fœtuses deposited.	Ten years. 1836–1845.	Nine years. 1846–1854.
From 2 to 3 months	21	58
„ 3 to 4 „	35	73
„ 4 to 5 „	56	102
„ 5 to 6 „	69	82
Total	181	315

Part of this advance, it is true, is attributable to the increase in the population of Paris, and in the prevalence of criminal abortion; but in great measure it is clearly owing to the enforcement of a more rigid law against secret burials. The above remarks are strikingly corroborated by the fact that of trials for the crime,—and we must not forget that these bear but a small ratio to the whole number of cases preliminarily investigated,[1] — there were in France, during the latter of these periods, fully four times the number occurring from 1836 to 1845.

The establishment of foundling hospitals, by the State governments, has been urged as a preventive of the crime; and, on the other hand, fears have been expressed lest the same means should increase it. For ourselves, however, and from some experience in such cases, we believe that these fears are groundless, and that with equal justice might they be entertained of every large charity having for its end the improvement, sanitary or otherwise, of the masses of society.[2]

We have a statute in Massachusetts, though practically unenforced, against one great agent in the increase of abortion, —an abuse of its license by the public press. Were such laws to become general, and to be faithfully executed, and were it also made penal to sell any drug,

[1] From 1846 to 1850, 188 cases of criminal abortion were discovered in Paris; but, for want of proof, only 22 of them were sent to trial. (Comptes Rendus Annuelles de la Justice Criminelle.)

[2] The recent establishment of a State asylum for infants in Massachusetts will soon practically test this question upon a sufficiently extensive scale.

popularly known as emmenagogue, except as advised by physicians, just as the sale of direct poisons is, or should be, controlled by law, the present system of openly advertising by abortionists would undoubtedly be brought to a close.

In no matter is it of more importance than in cases of suspected criminal abortion, that coroners should be intelligent and well-educated medical men; and we could wish that this point might have received especial attention from Dr. Semmes, in his report upon the subject to the American Medical Association.[1] In the sudden excitement of an inquest, the guilty are more likely than at a later period to be off their guard; and evidence may often be elicited at this time, which, at the subsequent trial, it would be impossible to obtain. There can be no question of the importance of this point; the coroner should be skilled in all that pertains to obstetric jurisprudence; and if similar knowledge were more generally possessed by other officers of justice, attorney, juror, and judge, a far greater number of convictions, under a proper law, would be secured.

As regards the more direct statutes, we shall hereafter consider their important points.

"In order to render laws effectually preventive," has wisely been said, "they should be consistently framed, and based on justice."[2] In accordance with this truly axiomatic doctrine, and with various rulings of the courts, no proof should be demanded which is not necessitated by the actual character of the crime. We have seen that neither in intent nor in fact is this an attempt against the person or life of the mother. If she die in consequence, the offender is already amenable for it as homicide, — in the absence of any special statute, at common law. The crime, both in intent and in fact, is against the life of the child.

The attempt being proved, it is unnecessary that it should have been consummated; not merely the completion of a crime

[1] Report on the Medico-legal Duties of Coroner. 1857.

[2] RADFORD, British Record of Obstetric Medicine, vol. i. p. 55.

bringing its punishment, but also certain overt acts with intent to the perpetration ; nor is it requisite that any injury, specific or general, should have been inflicted upon the person of the mother.

The offence being of equal guilt throughout pregnancy, proof of quickening — the incident, not the inception, of vitality, indicating neither the commencement of a new stage of existence, nor an advance from one stage to another,[1] and therefore an element without the slightest intrinsic value, — should not be required.

The crime of abortion should be considered to include, as it does in the absolute fact of moral guilt, all cases of attempted or intentionally effected destruction and miscarriage of the product of impregnation; and this, whether it be living or dead, normal or abnormal; which last expression equally comprehends instances of moles, hydatids, extra-uterine conception, acephalous, anencephalous, and other monsters.

Proof should not, as is now, in some States, by statute, be required of intent to destroy the child.[2] This should be considered shown by the intent to produce miscarriage, in the absence of lawful justification therefor; the act in all stages of pregnancy being attended with great danger to the child, and, in much more than a moiety of the period, necessarily fatal to it.

When the attempt is made criminal by statute, it follows, that proof of pregnancy is not necessary, and that conviction should be had though it were proved that pregnancy did not exist,[3] even that the woman on whom the abortion was attempted, however unlikely, was still a virgin.[4]

No discrimination should be made as to the means criminally employed, and an escape thus afforded to the

1 WHARTON, Crim. Law, § 1226, 5th ed.
2 Smith *v.* The State, 33 Maine (3 RED.), 48.
3 Regina *v.* Goodhall, 1 Denison C. C. 187.
4 TAYLOR, Medical Jurisprudence, p. 386.

guilty; as still obtains in Great Britain and many of our own States.

The mother, almost always an accessory before the fact, or the principal, should not, as now, be allowed almost perfect impunity. There is no valid reason for such entire exemption, unless we allow that all pregnant women are from that very fact more or less insane. There should be a certain measure of punishment for the mother, even if it be not so severe as for other parties engaged. The woman is covered by the laws of most nations of Continental Europe, — France, Austria, Germany, Bavaria, and Italy, — and by many of them her punishment, if married, is greatly increased. Similar severity is also exercised in these countries against the father of the fœtus, if he too is implicated in the crime.

To allow that abortion is extenuated in the unmarried, it has been said, will "to the moral and political philosopher appear to have exalted the sense of shame into the principle of virtue, and to have mistaken the great end of penal law, which is not vengeance, but the prevention of crime. Law, which is the guardian and bulwark of the public weal, must maintain a steady and even rigid watch over the general tendencies of human actions."[1] But, on the other hand, "the measure of punishment should be proportionate, as nearly as possible, to the temptation to offend, and to the kind and degree of evil produced by the offence."[2]

We have seen the increase in moral guilt, and of opportunity for commission and for escape, in the case of nurses, midwives, and other classes of persons, who, from their profession, are brought more directly into contact with pregnant women. By the penal code of Napoleon I., remarkable in so many respects for the wisdom of its provisions, an increase of punishment was enacted for abortion criminally induced or advised by physicians, surgeons, or other officers of health, including midwives, or by druggists;[3]

[1] Percival, Medical Ethics, p. 84. [2] Ibid., p. 85.
[3] Loc. cit., article 317.

their guilt being enhanced by their greater opportunities and knowledge.

Punishments for the crime of abortion should not, as is now generally the case, be so framed as to render the statute, in fact, if not in name, simply nugatory. Were the murder of adults to be made answerable by merely a year or two in prison, far more convictions than at present would undoubtedly be secured; but it is certain that the instances of the crime would be fearfully increased. We have reason to believe that it is precisely thus with the case in hand.

A standard of justification for the instances of necessary abortion should be fixed by law. If perfection in this respect be impossible, let the nearest approach be made to it that can.

Since our remarks upon the relative rights of the mother and fœtus to the chance of life in doubtful cases were first published, we have received from Rattenmann, late of Tübingen, an essay, written by himself, in which this question is discussed at length, and the repetition of abortion upon the same individual, in the early months of pregnancy, is defended. We have carefully considered the several arguments advanced by the gentleman, and are compelled to adhere to the views we have already expressed.

In presenting a report upon the matter, in 1857, by direction of the Suffolk District Medical Society of Massachusetts, the writer offered the draft of a law, prepared after much thought and consultation with legal as well as with medical men, and embodying the suggestions made above. This was intended for the consideration of the Legislature of the State, in the hope that it might be of aid toward a modification of the present defective law.

The report closed as follows: "We have aimed at a statute, which, while it better defined this atrocious crime, and covered the usual grounds of escape from conviction, established also the proper standard of competence in all medical questions involving issues of life and death. We believe that it would be the means of preventing much of the present awful waste of human life. But enforce such a law, and the profession would never allow its then high place in the community to be unworthily degraded; nor, as now, would those be permitted, unchallenged, to remain in fellowship, who were generally believed guilty, or suspected even of this crime."[1]

In the same belief, — strengthened by nearly eleven years' careful reflection, — that criminal abortion can, to a great extent, be controlled by law, if but the community so will, we proceed to the purely legal relations of the subject.

[1] Report to Suffolk District Medical Society, May, 1857, p. 12.

Two years later, as we have already stated, and in consequence of the action indicated above, the memorial of the American Medical Association, to which we have referred, was sent to the legislatures of the several States. There is reason to believe that, directly and indirectly, it was productive of a great deal of good.

CRIMINAL ABORTION.

BOOK II.

BOOK II.

FROM THE STAND-POINT OF LAW.

CHAPTER I.

THE COMMON LAW.

IN the well-known Latin work called "FLETA,"[1] the law is thus stated, lib. I. cap. 23: —

§ 10. Qui etiam mulierem prægnantem oppresserit, vel venenum dederit vel percusserit ut faciat abortivum, vel non concipiat, si fœtus erat jam formatus et animatus, rectè homicida est. § 11. Et similiter qui dederit vel acceperit venenum sub hâc intentione ne fiat generatio vel conceptio. § 12. Item facit homicidium mulier quæ puerum animatum per potationem et hujusmodi in ventre devastaverit.

[1] FLETA; seu Commentarius Juris Anglicani, sub Edwardo I. ab anonymo conscriptus: editus, cum dissertatione historicâ ad eundem, per Jo. Seldenum. This is a commentary in Latin, on the entire body of the English Law, as it stood at the time when the author wrote, which is supposed by some authorities to have been as late as the reign of Edward II. or Edward III.; but it has been satisfactorily shown by SELDEN, that it also belongs to the time of Edward I. The author is unknown, and gives as a reason for the title of his book, that it was written during his confinement in the Fleet Prison. His design seems to have been to give a concise account of the law, with such alterations as had been made since the time of BRACTON, to whose treatise his work thus serves as an appendix and often as a commentary. The work was first published by SELDEN in 1647, 4to., with a learned dissertation by SELDEN himself. Another edition was published in 1685, 4to., but no others have been printed in England. See SPILSBURY's Lincoln's Inn and Library, p. 162: Introduction to NICHOLS's ed. BRITTON, I. xxv. Oxford, 1865.

We give the following translation of this remarkable passage, which must have been written about A.D. 1290: —

Moreover, whoever shall have overlain a pregnant woman, or who shall have given her drugs or blows, in such sort as to procure abortion, or non-conception after the fœtus shall have been already formed and endowed with life, is, by law, a homicide: And in like manner, whoever shall have given or taken drugs to the intent that no generation or conception may take place: Also the woman doeth homicide, who, by potions and things of that sort, shall have destroyed her animate child in her womb.

Strange as it may seem, this third and last proposition of FLETA does not seem to have been recognized in the English law, although the English text-books and "books of Reports" are silent, or nearly so, on the subject, until the statute 24 & 25 Vict. ch. 100, § 58, which enacts that, "Every woman, being with child, who, with intent to procure her own miscarriage, shall unlawfully administer to herself any poison or other noxious thing, or shall unlawfully use any instrument or other means whatsoever, with like intent, shall be guilty of felony." And it is to be observed, that FLETA states that the destruction of the child is not only felony, but *homicide;* an offence not against the mother, whether directly or indirectly, but against the child. The more modern doctrine of the common law seems to have been based on the first and second propositions.

In the latest text-book on the Criminal Law published in England,[1] it is laid down that "an infant in its mother's womb, not being in rerum naturâ, is not considered as a person who can be killed, within the description of murder;[2] and therefore, if a woman, being quick or great with child, take any potion to cause an abortion, or if another give her

[1] RUSSELL on Crimes, I. 670, 4th ed. 1865.

[2] In BRITTON this reason is assigned: "For an infant killed within her womb, a woman may not bring any appeal, no one being bound to answer to an appeal of felony when the plaintiff cannot set forth the name of the person against whom the felony was committed." Liv. I. ch. xxiv. § 7, NICHOLS's ed. I. 114, Oxford, 1865.

any such potion, or if a person strike her, whereby the child within her is killed, it is not murder or manslaughter." But, by the above quoted statute, any person unlawfully administering poison, or other noxious thing, to procure the miscarriage of any woman, or unlawfully using any instrument, or other means whatsoever, with the like intent, is guilty of felony. In many of the United States, it is a felony if the woman dies; otherwise, it is a misdemeanor.

Where a child, having been born alive, afterwards died by reason of any potions or bruises it received in the womb, it seems always to have been the better opinion that it was murder in such as administered or gave them.[1] Giving a child, whilst in the act of being born, a mortal wound in the head as soon as the head appears, and before the child has breathed, will, if the child is afterwards born alive, and dies thereof, and there is malice, be murder; but, if there is not malice, manslaughter.

The prisoner was indicted for the manslaughter of an infant child; he practised midwifery, and was called in to attend a woman who was taken in labor; and when the head of the child became visible, being grossly ignorant of the art which he professed, and unable to deliver the woman with safety to herself and the child, as might have been done by a person of ordinary skill, he broke and compressed the skull of the infant, and thereby occasioned its death immediately after it was born. It was submitted, that the indictment was misconceived, though the facts would warrant an indictment in another form; and that, the child being *en ventre sa mère* at the time the wound was given, the prisoner could not be guilty of manslaughter;

[1] Inst. III. 50. HAWKINS P. C. I. ch. 31, § 16. BL. Comm. IV. 198. EAST P. C. ch. 5, § 14, I. p. 228. *Contra*, HALE P. C. I. 432, and STAUNDFORDE, 21. But the reason on which the opinions of the two last writers seem to be founded — namely, the difficulty of ascertaining the fact — cannot be considered as satisfactory, unless it be supposed that such fact never can be clearly established. See Exod. ch. xxi. v. 22, 23. RUSSELL on Crimes, I. 671, and note.

but, having been found guilty, the judges, upon a case reserved, were unanimously of opinion that the conviction was right.[1]

If a person, intending to procure abortion, causes a child to be born so soon that it cannot live, and it dies in consequence, this is murder, though no bodily injury be inflicted on the child. Upon the trial of an indictment against Ann West for murder, it appeared that S. Henson, being with child, went to the prisoner, and underwent an operation for the purpose of procuring abortion. This operation was repeated on several days, and Henson was shortly after delivered of a male child, she being then about six months advanced in her pregnancy. The child was born alive, but died about five hours afterwards. A medical witness stated that there were no unusual appearances on the child, and that it was a healthy child; but that, being born at that period of gestation, it was impossible that it could live any considerable length of time separated from the womb of its mother. The witness added: "Judging from the healthy appearance of the child, I cannot suppose that the premature delivery was spontaneous. The operations described by Henson would naturally and probably produce that premature delivery. It might be produced by a fall, or any sudden shock received by the mother; but, in this case, I have no doubt it was produced by the acts of the prisoner."[2] MAULE J. told the jury, that if a person, intending to procure abortion, does an act which causes a child to be born so much earlier than the natural time, that it is born in a state much less capable of living, and afterwards dies in consequence of its exposure to the external world, the person who by her misconduct so brings the child into the world, and puts it thereby into a situation in which it cannot live, is guilty of murder. The evidence seems to show clearly that the death of the

[1] Rex *v.* Senior, 1 Moody C. C. 346 (1832).

[2] The indictment alleged that the prisoner forced his right hand and a pin into the womb of Henson; and the report states that the operation was "of the nature described in the indictment."

child was caused by its premature birth; and, if that premature delivery was brought on by the felonious act of the prisoner, then the offence is complete. If the child, by the felonious act of the prisoner, was brought into the world in a state in which it was more likely to die than it would have been if born in due time, and did die in consequence, the offence is murder; and the mere existence of a possibility that something might have been done to prevent the death, would not render it less murder.[1]

Questions of considerable nicety sometimes arise on trials for infanticide, — as to whether the death took place after the child was actually born, or whilst it was in the progress of being born; and, although the law be clear that a child must be actually born to be the subject of murder, perhaps it is not clearly settled what constitutes actual birth for this purpose. Where, on the trial of an indictment alleging that the prisoner was delivered of a child, and that she afterwards strangled it, it appeared that the child, which was found concealed, had breathed; but the medical men could not say whether it had breathed during the birth or afterwards, — LITTLEDALE J. said to the jury, "The being born must mean that the whole body is brought into the world; and it is not sufficient that the child respires in the progress of the birth."[2]

So where, upon the trial of an indictment containing a count for murder by stabbing, and a count charging, that, before the child was completely born, the prisoner stabbed it with a fork, and that it was born, and then died of the stab, it was proved that a puncture was found on the child's skull; but when that injury was inflicted did not appear, and some questions were asked as to whether the child had breathed, — PARKE J. said: "The child might breathe before it was born; but its having breathed is not sufficiently life

[1] Regina v. West, 2 C. & K. 784 (1848). For the indictment in this case, see the Appendix to this volume.

[2] Rex v. Poulton, 5 C. & P. 329 (1832).

to make the killing of the child murder. There must have been an independent circulation in the child, or the child cannot be considered as alive for this purpose."[1]

So where the first count of an indictment charged that the prisoner, being big with a female child, did bring forth the said child alive, and did afterwards strangle it, and other counts varied the statement of the mode of death, but all of them stated the birth of the child as above mentioned; and it appeared that the dead body of the child was found concealed under the prisoner's bed, with a ribbon tied tightly round the neck, and the evidence of the medical witnesses left it in doubt whether the ribbon was tied round the neck, and the child strangled by it, during the progress of birth, or after the child was fully born, but before the umbilical cord was severed: and it was submitted, that a child could not be the subject of murder till it had a completely independent circulation, and had been wholly detached from the mother; that the term "born alive" meant the being completely separated from the mother, and having a completely independent circulation; and a child would not have an independent circulation for some time after it was completely brought forth, unless the umbilical cord was divided,— PARKE B. said: "It has been frequently so said in cases where the death has been caused by suffocation, or other injuries, which might have occurred in the course of unassisted delivery; but I should like to know whether there is any case where it has been so held, where a wilful wound has been inflicted during the birth of a child.[2] At all events, this indictment will not be supported, unless it be shown that the child was completely born, as it is distinctly averred that the child was brought forth before it was strangled." And, in summing up, the learned Baron said: "Whether there might be any question on a count differently framed,

[1] Rex v. Enock, 5 C. & P. 539 (1833). Regina v. Wright, 9 C. & P. 754 (1841), GURNEY B. s. P.

[2] See Rex v. Sellis, 7 C. & P. 850, *post* p. 158.

it is not necessary to say. Perhaps there might not; but, in order to convict on the first count, you must be satisfied that the whole body of the child had come forth from the body of the mother when the ligature was applied. If you think that the child was not killed after it came forth, you will acquit. I think it is essential that it should have been wholly produced. But supposing you should be of opinion that the child was strangled intentionally while it was connected by the umbilical cord to the mother, and after it was wholly produced, in that case I should put the matter into a course of further inquiry, directing you to convict the prisoner, and reserving the point for a higher tribunal; my present impression being, that it would be murder, if those were the facts of the case."[1]

And in a subsequent case, where this case was mentioned, and the prisoner's counsel admitted that it did not go to the length of deciding that the child must have a separate, independent existence from that of the mother in order to make the killing of it murder, VAUGHAN J. said, "I should have been very much surprised if it had; because, if that were the law, the child and the afterbirth might be completely delivered, and yet, because the umbilical cord was not separated, the child might be knocked on the head and killed, without the party who did it being guilty of murder."[2]

And where one count charged that the prisoner, being big with a female child, "*did bring forth the same alive*," and then, in the usual manner, alleged the murder of the child by choking it with a handkerchief; and another count charged the murder in the same way of a certain illegitimate child, "then lately before born of the body" of M. T.; and there was strong evidence to prove that the child had been wholly produced alive from the prisoner's body, and that

[1] Rex *v.* Crutchley, 7 C. & P. 814 (1837). The prisoner was acquitted of murder.

[2] Regina *v.* Reeves, 9 C. & P. 25 (1839).

she had strangled it; but it was also clearly proved, by the surgeon who examined the body of the child, that it must have been strangled before it had been separated from the mother by the severance of the umbilical cord; and the surgeon further stated that a child has, after breathing fully, an independent circulation of its own, even while still attached to the mother by the umbilical cord, and that, in his judgment, the child in question had breathed fully after it had been wholly produced, and had therefore an independent circulation of its own before and at the time it was strangled, and was then in a state to carry on a separate existence,—ERSKINE J. directed the jury, that if they were satisfied that the child had been wholly produced from the body of the prisoner alive, and that the prisoner wilfully strangled the child after it had been so produced, and while it was alive, and while it had, according to the evidence of the surgeon, an independent circulation of its own, he was of opinion that the charge in the said counts was made out, although the child, at the time it was so strangled, still remained attached to the mother by the navel-string. The jury found the prisoner guilty; and, upon a case reserved, the judges held the conviction right.[1]

Where the prisoner was indicted for the murder of her child by cutting off its head, and a surgeon stated that he was enabled to say decidedly that the child had breathed, but he could not swear that the whole body of the child was born when the act of breathing took place, COLTMAN J. said: "In order to justify a conviction for murder, you must be satisfied that the entire child was actually born into the world in a living state. The fact of its having breathed is not a decisive proof that it was born alive; it may have breathed, and yet died before birth."[2]

But, if a child be actually wholly produced alive, it is not necessary that it should have breathed, to make it the sub-

1 Regina *v.* Trilloe, 2 Moody C. C. 260, and C. & Marsh. 650 (1842).

2 Rex *v.* Sellis, 7 C. & P. 850 (1837).

ject of murder. Upon an indictment for the murder of a child, where it appeared that the dead body of the child was found in a river, and it was proved by two surgeons that it had never breathed, PARK J. said, "A child must be actually wholly in the world in a living state to be the subject of a charge of murder; but, if it has been wholly born, and is alive, it is not essential that it should have breathed at the time it was killed, as many children are born alive, and yet do not breathe for some time after their birth."[1]

We have thus stated at length the cases on this branch of the law of infanticide, for the reason that an indictment for administering drugs or using instruments for the purpose of producing abortion may be so framed, and the evidence may be such, that the questions which are there discussed may be of vital importance. But it must be observed, that some of these cases are unsatisfactory, as many rulings at *nisi prius* must necessarily be.

It is a general principle, that if an action unlawful in itself be done deliberately, and with intention of mischief or great bodily harm to particular individuals, or of mischief indiscriminately, fall where it may, and death ensue against or beside the original intention of the party, it will be murder. Thus, where a person gave medicine to a woman to procure an abortion,[2] and where a person put skewers into the womb of a woman for the same purpose,[3] by which, in both cases, the women were killed, these acts were held clearly to be murder; for, though the death of the woman was not intended, the acts were of a nature deliberate and malicious, and necessarily attended with great danger to the persons on whom they were practised.[4]

1 Rex *v.* Brain, 6 C. & P. 349 (1834).

2 HALE P. C. I. 429.

3 Tinckler's Case, EAST P. C. I. ch. v. § 17, I. p. 230, and § 124, p. 354 (1781).

4 RUSSELL on Crimes, I. 740.

In some of the United States, it has been decided that it is not a punishable offence, by the common law, to perform an operation upon a pregnant woman, with her consent, for the purpose of procuring an abortion, and thereby to effect such purpose, unless the woman is quick with child.[1] "Such a distinction," says a writer on the criminal law, "is neither in accordance with the result of medical experience, nor with the principles of the criminal law."[2]

In Pennsylvania, a contrary doctrine has been held. Said Mr. Justice COULTER: "It is not the murder of a living child which constitutes the offence, but the destruction of gestation by wicked means and against nature. The moment the womb is instinct with embryo life, and gestation has begun, the crime may be perpetrated."[3] "If we look at the reason of the law," writes Mr. BISHOP, "we shall prefer the Pennsylvania doctrine, because the public and private mischiefs are the same, whether the abortion takes place just before or just after the first movings of the coming human existence are perceptible to the expectant mother."[4]

There is a precedent in CHITTY'S Criminal Law,[5] which is an indictment at common law, in which it is not alleged that the woman was quick with child. It does not appear that any judgment was rendered on this indictment, which was procured from the Crown Office, Michaelmas Term 42

1 Commonwealth *v.* Parker, 9 Met. 263 (1845), explaining Commonwealth *v.* Bangs, 9 Mass. 387 (1812). The State *v.* Cooper, 2 Zabriskie, 52 (1849). Smith *v.* The State, 32 Maine, 48 (1851). See the argument of the counsel for the defendant, in Hall *v.* Hancock, 15 Pick. 256 (1834). The act was purged of its criminality, so far as it affected the mother, by her consent. It was an offence against the life of the child. The State *v.* Murphy, 3 Dutcher, 114 (1858).

2 WHARTON Crim. Law, I. § 1220, 5th ed.

3 Mills *v.* Commonwealth, 13 Pennsylvania State Rep. 631 (1850). See the earlier case, Commonwealth *v.* Demain, decided by the Supreme Court of Pennsylvania, January Term 1846, and reported in 6 Pennsylvania Law Journal, 29, and in Brightly, 441. And see a criticism on this case in The State *v.* Cooper, 2 Zabriskie, 58 (1849).

4 Comm. Crim. Law, II. § 6.

5 Vol. III. p. 798. This precedent is printed in the Appendix to this volume.

Geo. III. The next year, Lord ELLENBOROUGH'S Act was passed, declaring the procuring of an abortion, though the woman is not quick with child, a felony. Upon a careful consideration of this precedent, it will not be found inconsistent with the rule of the common law, — that, until the woman is quick with child, if she consents, no indictable offence is committed. The indictment contains several counts, and they all charge an assault upon the woman; and there is no intimation that the applications were made with her consent; but the conclusion from the averments is otherwise. It is then the case of an assault at common law, with aggravations. But what is more material is, that, although the woman was not alleged to be quick with child, yet it is averred that she was pregnant and big with child, and that the act was done by the defendant wilfully, and with intent feloniously, wilfully, and of his malice aforethought, to kill and murder the child with which she was so big and pregnant; and, in other counts, it is laid that drugs were administered to her, she being pregnant with another child, and with intent to cause and procure her to miscarry, and bring forth said child dead, &c. The whole proceeds on the averment, that she was then pregnant with a child then so far advanced as to be regarded in law as having a separate existence, a life capable of being destroyed; which is equivalent to the averment that she was quick with child.[1]

"Care must be taken," said Chief Justice SHAW,[2] "not to confound this case [i.e., whether, before the fœtus has quickened, an abortion procured with the mother's consent is an offence at common law] with some others, which resemble it in fact, but fall within another principle. The use of violence upon a woman, with an intent to procure her miscarriage without her consent, is an assault highly aggravated by such wicked purpose, and would be indictable at com-

[1] Commonwealth v. Parker, 9 Met. 265 (1845). The State v. Cooper, 2 Zabriskie, 56 (1849).

[2] Commonwealth v. Parker, 9 Met. 265 (1845).

mon law. So where, upon a similar attempt by drugs or instruments, the death of the mother ensues, the party making such an attempt, with or without the consent of the woman, is guilty of the murder of the mother, on the ground that it is an act done without lawful purpose, dangerous to life, and that the consent of the woman cannot take away the imputation of malice, any more than in case of a duel, where, in like manner, there is the consent of the parties."

The words, "quick with child," have been variously construed. In *Rex* v. *Phillips*,[1] upon an indictment on 43 Geo. III. ch. 58, § 2, for endeavoring to procure an abortion, where it appeared that the woman was in the fourth month of her pregnancy, but swore she had not felt the child move within her before the taking the medicine, and that she was not then quick with child; and where the medical men, in their examinations, differed as to the time when the fœtus may be stated to be quick, and to have a distinct existence, but all agreed, that, in common understanding, a woman is not to be considered quick with child till she has felt the child alive and quick within her, which happens with different women in different stages of pregnancy, although most usually about the fifteenth or sixteenth week after conception, — LAWRENCE J. said, that this was the interpretation that must be put upon the words, "quick with child," in the statute; and, as the woman had not felt the child alive within her before taking the medicine, he directed the jury to acquit the prisoner. In an investigation before a jury of matrons, Mr. Baron GURNEY said, "'Quick with child' is having conceived. 'With quick child' is when the child has quickened."[2] But the distinction between these expressions has been denied. "There is no foundation whatever in law for this distinction," said Chief Justice

1 3 Campb. 77 (1811). 9 Met. 266.

2 Regina *v.* Wycherly, 8 C. & P. 262, 264 (1838.) See a note to this case, by the reporters, showing, on medical authority, that the popular idea of quick or not quick with child is founded in error.

GREEN: "The ancient authorities show clearly that the terms are synonymous; both importing that the child had quickened in the womb, and that the period had arrived when the life of the infant, in contemplation of law, had commenced."[1]

In Ohio, a statute enacts, "That any physician or other person, who shall wilfully administer to any pregnant woman any medicine, drug, substance, or thing whatever, with intent thereby to procure the miscarriage of any such woman, unless the same shall have been necessary to preserve the life of such woman, or shall have been advised by two physicians to be necessary for that purpose, shall, upon conviction, be punished," etc. It has been decided that the offence may be committed at any time during the period of gestation.[2] And in Vermont, where it is a statutory offence to attempt to procure the miscarriage of a woman "then pregnant with child," it has been held not to be essential that the fœtus be alive at the time the attempt is made. "We think," said REDFIELD C.J. "the mother is with child, whether the child be dead or alive, until the actual miscarriage by the expulsion of the fœtus."[3]

In Hall *v.* Hancock,[4] the court were of opinion, that the distinction between a woman being pregnant, and being quick with child, is applicable mainly, if not exclusively, to criminal cases; and that it does not apply to cases of descents, devises, and other gifts; and that, generally, a child will be considered in being from conception to the time of its birth, in all cases where it will be for the benefit of such child to be so considered.

The Massachusetts statute of 1845, ch. 27, enacts, that "Whoever maliciously, or without lawful justification, with intent to cause and procure the miscarriage of a woman then pregnant with child, shall," etc. On the trial of an indict-

[1] The State *v.* Cooper, 2 Zabriskie, 57 (1849). BISHOP Crim. Law, II. § 7.

[2] Wilson *v.* The State, 2 Ohio State, 319 (1853).

[3] The State *v.* Howard, 32 Vermont, 380, 403 (1859). BISHOP Crim. Law, II. § 8.

[4] 15 Pick. 255 (1834).

ment under the statute, the court was requested to instruct the jury that a lawful justification would exist "if the child with which the woman was pregnant was not a live child." "If," said THOMAS J. "by this was meant that the mother had not reached the stage of pregnancy in which she would be 'quick with child,' and when to procure an abortion would be an offence at common law, the prayer, in our opinion, misconceives the purpose of the statute, which was intended to supply the defects of the common law, and to apply to all cases of pregnancy. If the defendant meant to say it would be a legal justification to show that the fœtus with which the woman was pregnant had lost its vitality, so that it could never mature into a living child, we think the position correct."[1]

It seems, that pregnancy ceases when the child has come forth from the womb of the mother, though the child is still attached by the umbilical cord, and though the afterbirth has not been removed.[2]

[1] Commonwealth *v.* Wood, 11 Gray, 86 (1858).

[2] Commonwealth *v.* Brown, 14 Gray, 419 (1860).

CHAPTER II.

THE ENGLISH STATUTES AND INDICTMENTS THEREON.

IN England, the statutes 43 Geo. III. ch. 58, 9 Geo. IV. ch. 31, and 7 Will. IV. and 1 Vict. ch. 85, formerly made certain attempts to procure the miscarriage of any woman highly penal; but these acts are repealed, and the recent act, 24 & 25 Vict. ch. 100, §§ 58, 59, is in force. These statutes are printed in this chapter, for the reason that they have been re-enacted, with alterations and additions, in many of the United States. For the assistance of the practitioner in framing an indictment under the particular statute of his own State, precedents of indictments have been inserted, drawn on these English statutes.

The first section of 43 Geo. III. ch. 58, known as Lord ELLENBOROUGH'S Act, after reciting that certain heinous offences, with intent to procure the miscarriage of women, had been of late frequently committed, and that no adequate means had been provided for their prevention and punishment, enacts, that if any person or persons "shall wilfully, maliciously, and unlawfully administer to, or cause to be administered to or taken by any of his Majesty's subjects, any deadly poison, or other noxious and destructive substance or thing, with intent such his Majesty's subjects thereby to murder, or thereby to cause and procure the miscarriage of any woman, then being quick with child," the person or persons so offending, their counsellors, aiders, and abettors, knowing of and privy to such offence, shall be felons, and shall suffer death, as in cases of felony, without benefit of clergy.

The second section of the statute recites, that it might sometimes happen that poison or some other noxious and destructive substance or thing might be given, or other means used, with intent to procure miscarriage or abortion, where the woman might not be quick with child at the time, or it might not be proved that she was quick with child; and enacts, "That if any person or persons shall wilfully and maliciously administer to, or cause to be administered to, or taken by any woman, any medicine, drug, or other substance or thing whatsoever, or shall use, employ, or cause, or procure to be used or employed, any instrument or other means whatsoever, with intent thereby to cause or procure the miscarriage of any woman not being, or not being proved to be, quick with child at the time of administering such things, or using such means, that then and in every such case, the person or persons so offending, their counsellors, aiders, and abettors, knowing of and privy to such offence, shall be and are hereby declared to be guilty of felony, and shall be liable to be fined, imprisoned, set in and upon the pillory, publicly or privately whipped, or to suffer one or more of the said punishments, or to be transported beyond the seas, for any term not exceeding fourteen years, at the discretion of the court, before which such offender shall be tried and convicted."

Indictment for administering drugs to procure abortion, the woman not being quick with child. 43 Geo. III. ch. 58, § 2.[1]

The jurors, etc., upon their oath present, that J. S. late of B. in the county of M. laborer, on the first day of June in the year of our Lord ——, at B. aforesaid in the county aforesaid, feloniously, wilfully, and maliciously did administer to, and cause to be administered to and taken by one A. N., a large quantity of a certain drug called savin, to wit, two ounces of the said drug, with intent then and there and thereby to cause and procure the miscarriage of the said A. N., she the said A. N. at the time of the administering and taking the said drug as aforesaid, being with child, but not quick with child, to wit, at B. aforesaid, in the county afore-

[1] ARCHBOLD Crim. Pl. (2d London ed.) 235.

said; against the form of the statute in such case made and provided, and against the peace, etc.

Add a second count, substituting for the words, "being with child, but not quick with child," the words, "not being quick with child."

Add also another set of counts, charging the defendant with having administered, etc., "a large quantity of a certain mixture to the jurors aforesaid unknown."

Indictment if the woman were quick with child. 43 Geo. III. ch. 58, § 1.[1]

[*Commencement as in the last precedent.*] in the county aforesaid, feloniously, wilfully, maliciously, and unlawfully did administer to, and cause to be administered to and taken by one A. N., a large quantity of a certain noxious and destructive substance called savin, to wit, two ounces of the said substance called savin, with intent then and there and thereby to cause and procure the miscarriage of the said A. N., she the said A. N., at the time of the administering and taking the said substance as aforesaid, being quick with child, to wit, at B. aforesaid, in the county aforesaid: against the form of the statute in such case made and provided, and against the peace, etc.

The 9 Geo. IV. ch. 31, Lord LANSDOWNE'S Act, enacts —

XIII. That, if any person, with intent to procure the miscarriage of any woman then being quick with child, unlawfully and maliciously shall administer to her, or cause to be taken by her, any poison or other noxious thing, or shall use any instrument or other means whatever with the like intent; every such offender, and every person counselling, aiding, or abetting such offender, shall be guilty of felony; and, being convicted thereof, shall suffer death as a felon; and if any person, with intent to procure the miscarriage of any woman not being or not being proved to be, then quick with child, unlawfully and maliciously shall administer to

[1] ARCHBOLD Crim. Pl. (2d London ed.) 236.

her, or cause to be taken by her, any medicine or other thing, or shall use any instrument or other means whatever, with the like intent; every such offender, and every person counselling, aiding, or abetting such offender, shall be guilty of felony, and being convicted thereof, shall be liable, at the discretion of the court, to be transported beyond the seas for any term not exceeding fourteen years nor less than seven years, or to be imprisoned, with or without hard labor, in the common gaol or house of correction, for any term not exceeding three years, and if a male, to be once, twice, or thrice publicly or privately whipped, (if the court shall so think fit) in addition to such imprisonment.

Indictment for procuring abortion when quick *with child.* 9 Geo. IV. ch. 31, § 13.

The jurors, etc., on their oath present, that C. D. late of B. in the county of S. physician, on the first day of June in the year of our Lord ——, at B. aforesaid, in the county aforesaid, feloniously, unlawfully, and maliciously did administer to, and cause to be taken by one E. F., she the said E. F. then and there being quick with child, a large quantity, to wit, two ounces of a certain noxious thing, to wit, a noxious thing called [savin] with intent then and there and thereby to procure the miscarriage of the said E. F.: contrary to the form of the statute in such case made and provided, and against the peace, etc.

Second count. — And the jurors aforesaid, upon their oath aforesaid, do further present, that the said C. D. on the day and year aforesaid, at B. aforesaid, in the county aforesaid, feloniously, unlawfully, and maliciously did administer to and cause to be taken by the said E. F., she the said E. F., then and there being quick with child, a large quantity, to wit, two ounces, of a certain poison and noxious thing to the jurors aforesaid unknown, with intent then and there and thereby to procure the miscarriage of the said E. F.: contrary to the form, etc.

Third count. — And the jurors aforesaid upon their oath aforesaid, do further present, that the said C. D. on the day and year aforesaid, at B. aforesaid in the county aforesaid, feloniously, unlawfully, and maliciously then and there did, with intent to procure the miscarriage of the said E. F., the said E. F. being then and there quick with child, use a certain instrument, to wit, a ——, in and upon the body of the said E. F., by then and there [*state how it was used*]: contrary to the form, etc.

Indictment for procuring abortion when not *quick with child.* 9 Geo. IV. ch. 31, § 13, second clause.

The jurors, etc., that C. D. late of B. in the county of S. physician on the first day of June, in the year of our Lord ——, at B. aforesaid in the county aforesaid, feloniously, unlawfully, and maliciously did administer to and cause to be taken by one E. F., she the said E. F. then and there being with child, but not quick with child, a large quantity, to wit [*proceed as in the preceding indictment to the end.*]

St. 7 Will. IV. & 1 Vict. ch. 85 enacts —

VI. Whosoever, with intent to procure the miscarriage of any woman, shall unlawfully administer to her, or cause to be taken by her, any poison or other noxious thing, or shall unlawfully use any instrument or other means whatsoever with the like intent, shall be guilty of felony, and being convicted thereof, shall be liable, at the discretion of the court, to be transported beyond the seas for the term of his or her natural life, or for any term not less than fifteen years, or to be imprisoned for any term not exceeding three years.

Indictment for administering poison to procure miscarriage. 7 Will. IV. & 1 Vict. ch. 85, § 6.[1]

The jurors, etc., upon their oath present, that C. D. late of B. in the county of S. laborer, on the first day of June

[1] ARCHBOLD Crim. Pl. (7th London ed.) 413.

in the year of our Lord ——, at B. aforesaid, in the county aforesaid, feloniously and unlawfully did administer to, and cause to be taken by, one E. F., a large quantity of a certain noxious thing called savin, to wit, two ounces of the said noxious thing called savin, with intent then and there and thereby to procure the miscarriage of the said E. F.: contrary to the form of the statute in such case made and provided, and against the peace, etc.

Indictment for using instruments to procure miscarriage. 7 Will. IV. & 1 Vict. ch. 85, § 6.[1]

[*Commencement as in the last precedent*] in the county aforesaid, feloniously and unlawfully did use a certain instrument, called a ——, by then and there [*state the mode of using the instrument*] with intent [*proceed as in the last precedent.*]

St. 24 & 25 Vict. ch. 100, enacts —

LVIII. Every woman, being with child, who, with intent to procure her own miscarriage, shall unlawfully administer to herself any poison or other noxious thing, or shall unlawfully use any instrument or other means whatsoever with the like intent, — and whosoever, with intent to procure the miscarriage of any woman, whether she be or be not with child, shall unlawfully[2] administer to her or cause to be taken by her, any poison or other noxious thing, or shall unlawfully[3] use any instrument or other means whatsoever with the like intent, — shall be guilty of felony, and being convicted thereof shall be liable, at the discretion of the court, to be kept in penal servitude for life or for any term not less than three years, — or to be imprisoned for any term not exceeding two years, with or without hard labor, and with or without solitary confinement.[4]

1 Archbold Crim. Pl. (7th London ed.) 414.

2 The word "maliciously" was in the 9 Geo. IV. ch. 31, § 13.

3 "Unlawfully" was not in the 9 Geo. IV. ch. 31, § 13.

4 This clause is framed on the 7 Will. IV. & 1 Vict. ch. 85, § 6. The first

LIX. Whosoever shall unlawfully supply or procure any poison or other noxious thing, or any instrument or thing whatsoever, knowing that the same is intended to be unlawfully used or employed with intent to procure the miscarriage of any woman, whether she be or be not with child, shall be guilty of a misdemeanor, and being convicted thereof, shall be liable, at the discretion of the court, to be kept in penal servitude for the term of three years, or to be imprisoned for any term not exceeding two years, with or without hard labor.[1]

Indictment for administering drugs, etc., to procure abortion. 24 & 25 Vict. ch. 100, § 58.

The jurors, etc., upon their oath present, that C. D. of B. in the county of S. on the first day of June, in the year of our Lord ——, at B. aforesaid in the county aforesaid, unlawfully and feloniously did administer to [*or* did cause to be taken by] a certain woman called E. F. a large quantity, to wit, —— of a certain noxious thing called ——, with intent then and there and thereby to cause the miscarriage of the said E. F.: against the form of the statute in such case made and provided, and against the peace, etc.

Indictment for using instruments to procure abortion. 24 & 25 Vict. ch. 100, § 58.

The jurors, etc., upon their oath present, that C. D. of B. in the county of S. on the first day of June, in the year of our Lord ——, at B. aforesaid, in the county aforesaid, unlawfully and feloniously did use a certain instrument called a ——, by then and there [*stating how it was used;* the

part of it is new, and extends the former enactment to any woman who, being with child, attempts to procure her own miscarriage. The second part in terms makes it immaterial whether the woman were or were not with child, in accordance with the decision in Regina *v.* Goodhall, 1 Denison C. C. 187; s.c. as Regina *v.* Goodchild, 2 C. & K. 293 (1846).

[1] This section is new. It is intended to check the obtaining of poison, etc., for the purpose of causing abortion, by making both the person who supplies and the person who procures it guilty of a misdemeanor.

words in the statute are, "any instrument or other means whatsoever;" *if by any other means state them*[1]]; with intent then and there and thereby to cause the miscarriage of the said E. F.: against the form of the statute in such case made and provided, and against the peace, etc.

Add another count, stating it to be "a certain instrument to the jurors aforesaid unknown." The name of the woman will be stated, in stating the manner in which the instrument was used, and referred to afterwards as "the said E. F."

1 See the indictment in Regina *v.* West, 2 C. & K. 784, in the Appendix to this volume.

CHAPTER III.

AGAINST WHOM AN INDICTMENT LIES. — PRINCIPALS AND ACCESSORIES.

It is a general principle in the criminal law, that where a statute enacts an offence to be felony, though it mentions nothing of accessories before or after, yet virtually and consequentially those that counsel or command the offence are accessories before the fact, and those who knowingly receive the offender are accessories after.[1] And every indictment for felony, whether it be a felony at common law or by statute, must allege that the act which forms the subject-matter of the indictment was done "feloniously;" the word "feloniously" being a term of art for which no equivalent expression can be substituted.[2]

The earliest English case on this subject is *Rex* v. *Russell*, decided in 1832.[3] Russell was tried on an indictment which charged S. Wormsley with murdering herself with arsenic, and Russell with inciting her to commit the said murder. It appeared that Wormsley, who was about four months advanced in pregnancy, but not quick with child, died from taking arsenic, which she had received from Russell for the purpose of procuring a miscarriage, and that she knowingly took it, with intent to procure a miscarriage, in the absence of Russell. It was objected, that there was no evidence to prove that she was felo de se; that the 9 Geo. IV. ch. 31, § 13,[4] did not apply to a woman administering poison to herself, and that assuming her to have taken

[1] Purcell Crim. Pl. 25.

[2] Regina *v.* Gray, Leigh & Cave C. C. 365; 9 Cox C. C. 437; 9 L. T. Rep. N. S. 808 (1864). Purcell Crim. Pl. 87.

[3] 1 Moody C. C. 356.

[4] Ante, p. 166.

arsenic knowingly, and with intent to procure miscarriage, she was not guilty of any offence; and, consequently, if there were no principal, there could be no accessory. It was held, that she was felo de se, and that Russell was an accessory before the fact.

In *Regina* v. *Gaylor*,[1] it appeared, that the prisoner procured sulphate of potash, and gave it to his wife, intending that she should take it for the purpose of procuring abortion; and that she, believing herself to be pregnant, although in reality she was not, took the sulphate of potash in the absence of the prisoner, and died from its effects. It was held that he was rightly convicted of manslaughter. ERLE J. reserved the following case: "The prisoner was indicted for manslaughter. The facts were, that his wife's death was caused by swallowing sulphate of potash for the purpose of procuring abortion; she believing herself to be pregnant, although in reality she was not. The prisoner purchased this sulphate of potash, and gave it to his wife in order that she might swallow it for the above-mentioned purpose; but he was absent at the time when she so swallowed it. For the prosecution it was contended, that the wife committed a felony in so swallowing the sulphate of potash, and, as death ensued therefrom, she also committed murder;[2] that the prisoner was an accessory before the fact, to this felony, and to the consequent murder, and might be tried as if the principal had been convicted under 11 & 12 Vict. ch. 46, § 1;[3] and that, although the evidence showed his offence was murder, yet that would support an indictment for manslaughter. Under my direction the jury convicted. I reserved the following questions: —

[1] Dearsly & Bell C. C. 288; 7 Cox C. C. 253 (1857).

[2] Rex *v.* Russell, 1 Moody C. C. 356 (1832). Ante, p. 172.

[3] That section enacts: "If any person shall become an accessory before the fact to any felony, whether the same be a felony at common law, or by virtue of any statute or statutes made or to be made, such person may be indicted, tried, convicted and punished in all respects as if he were a principal felon."

"1st. Was the deceased guilty of felony, in administering sulphate of potash to herself, for the purpose of procuring abortion, she not being pregnant? 2d. Was the husband, by his act, guilty of felony, or an accessory thereto? — he having been absent when she swallowed the drug. 3d. If the husband was an accessory to the felony, was an indictment for manslaughter supported? — it being laid down that there cannot be an accessory to manslaughter.[1] 4th. Can the indictment be supported under 11 & 12 Vict. ch. 46, § 1?" Judgment was given affirming the conviction, but no reasons were given. But it was undoubtedly affirmed on the ground, that the prisoner instigated the woman to take the drug.[2] In the course of the argument, BRAMWELL B. asked: "Suppose a man, for mischief, gives another a strong dose of medicine, not intending any further injury than causing him to be sick and uncomfortable, and death ensues, — would not that be manslaughter? Suppose, then, another had counselled him to do it, — would not he who counselled be an accessory before the fact?"[3] And ERLE J. said: "The man was an accessory before the fact, to the woman taking the drug with intent to procure abortion. This would in my opinion be murder, if she died in consequence of taking that drug. The grand jury, however, found that it was manslaughter. If a man is indicted for manslaughter, and it turns out to be murder, he may be found guilty of manslaughter. I thought the prisoner was guilty of murder, and might therefore be convicted of manslaughter."

In *Regina* v. *Fretwell*, the prisoner was induced by a woman who was pregnant by him, to get for her a dose of corrosive sublimate, for the purpose of producing abortion, which he did with a full knowledge of the purpose to which it was to be applied. The woman took the dose in the absence of the prisoner, and died in consequence. The jury found that the prisoner did not administer the poison to her, or cause her to

[1] HALE P. C. II. 437. [2] See the next case, Regina *v.* Fretwell.
[3] See Regina *v.* Smith, 2 Cox C. C. 233 (1847), per PARKE B.

take it. On a case reserved, it was held, that, even if the woman were felo de se, the prisoner could not be convicted of murder, either as a principal, or as an accessory before the fact.[1] The following case was reserved by COCKBURN C. J.: "Francis Fretwell was indicted and tried before me, at the last Assizes for the county of Nottingham, for the wilful murder of Elizabeth Bradley. The deceased had died from the effects of corrosive sublimate, taken for the purpose of producing abortion. The poison had been procured for her by the prisoner, with full knowledge of the purpose to which it was to be applied; but there was ground for believing that the prisoner, in procuring the poison, had acted at the instigation of the deceased, and under the influence of threats by her of self-destruction, if the means of producing abortion were not supplied to her. She was a married woman, living in service, separately from her husband, and had become pregnant by the prisoner. She had endeavored to purchase corrosive sublimate herself; but, the druggists to whom she had applied having refused to furnish it to her, she had urged the prisoner to procure it. The prisoner was not present when the poison was taken. The facts in question occurred in the month of July 1861, anterior to the coming into operation of the 24 & 25 Vict. ch. 100. The jury, upon questions specially put to them by me, upon the evidence, expressly negatived the fact of the prisoner having administered the poison to the deceased, or caused it to be taken by her. They found, specially, that the prisoner procured the poison, and delivered it to the deceased, with a knowledge of the purpose to which she intended to apply it, and that he was therefore accessory before the fact to her taking poison for the purpose of procuring abortion. Upon this finding, I directed the jury to return a verdict of wilful murder against the prisoner; reserving for the consideration and decision of the Court of Criminal Appeal the

1 Regina v. Fretwell, Leigh & Cave C. C. 161; 9 Cox. C. C. 152; 8 Jur. N. S. 466; 6 L. T. Rep. N. S. 333 (1862).

question, whether such verdict was right in point of law. In giving such direction, I acted in deference to the authority of the case of *Rex* v. *Russell;*[1] but it appearing to me doubtful how far the ruling of the judges in that case, that, if poison be taken by a woman to produce abortion, and death ensues, the woman is felo de se, could be upheld; and still more so, how far a man, accessory to the misdemeanor of a woman in taking poison for the purpose of producing abortion, can properly be held to be accessory to the self-murder of the woman, if, contrary to the intention of the parties, death should be the consequence, — I have reserved these points for the consideration of the court."

ERLE C. J.: "The prisoner was convicted of murder; and the question for us is, whether, upon the facts stated, he was properly convicted. The deceased, Elizabeth Bradley, was pregnant, and, for the purpose of producing abortion, took a dose of corrosive sublimate, which had been procured for her by the prisoner, with a full knowledge of the purpose to which it was to be applied. In procuring the poison, the prisoner had acted at the instigation of the deceased, and under the influence of threats by her of self-destruction, if the means of procuring abortion were not supplied to her. Then the case sets out the reasons which caused the woman to be so desirous of preventing her state becoming known. The jury expressly negatived the fact of the prisoner having administered the poison to the deceased, or caused it to be taken by her; but they found, that he had delivered it to her, with a knowledge of the purpose to which she intended to apply it, and that he was therefore accessory before the fact to her taking poison for the purpose of procuring abortion. Chief Justice COCKBURN thereupon, on the authority of *Russell's Case*, directed the jury to return a verdict of wilful murder against the prisoner, and reserved the case for the consideration of this Court. Now, upon the facts stated, the present case appears to me to differ materially

[1] 1 Moody C. C. 356 (1832). Ante, p. 172.

from that of *Rex* v. *Russell*. There the prisoner, finding the woman to be pregnant, of his own motion procured arsenic, gave it to the woman, and instigated and persuaded her to take it, for the purpose of procuring a miscarriage; and the woman took it knowingly, with the like intent of procuring a miscarriage, and thereby caused her own death. The judges held, that it was a misdemeanor in her to take arsenic for the purpose of procuring abortion; that, having thereby caused her own death, she was felo de se; and that the prisoner was an accessory before the fact to the murder. Now, there appears to me to be a very marked distinction between the conduct of the prisoner Fretwell, in this case, and the conduct of the prisoner Russell, in the case I have already referred to. In the latter case, Russell instigated and persuaded the woman to take the arsenic. In the present case, the prisoner was unwilling that the woman should take the poison. He procured it for her at her instigation, and under a threat by her of self-destruction. He did not administer it to her, or cause her to take it; and the facts of the case are quite consistent with the supposition, that he hoped and expected that she would change her mind, and would not resort to it. Then, the cases being distinguishable, it is unnecessary to decide whether in this case the woman was felo de se. I am the more fortified in my opinion by looking at the late statute for consolidating and amending the law relating to offences against the person.[1] By § 58 of that statute, any woman administering to herself poison with intent to procure miscarriage, and any person administering it to her, or causing it to be taken by her, with the like intent, is guilty of felony. By § 59, any one supplying or procuring any poison, knowing that the same is intended to be used with intent to procure miscarriage, is guilty of a misdemeanor. The crime, therefore, of procuring or supplying the poison, is one of a totally different character from that of administering it, or causing it to be taken. My

[1] 24 & 25 Vict. ch. 100. Ante, pp. 169, 170.

opinion is, that the prisoner was not guilty of murder, and that the conviction must be quashed."

MARTIN B.: "The acts of the prisoner were too remote from the death of the woman, to make him guilty of murder."

BLACKBURN J.: "According to the finding of the jury, the prisoner neither administered the poison, nor caused it to be taken by the woman, and therefore was not a party to what took place in such a way, as to [make what he did amount] to murder."

It seems, that an indictment, which avers that one defendant advised, ordered, and commanded two other defendants to administer ergot to a woman pregnant with child, and provided the ergot for the purpose, knowing that it was dangerous to life, which ergot she, according to his advice, order, and command swallowed; and that he, "in so ordering, advising, and commanding the said ergot administered to her," to be by her swallowed, it being for her provided by him as aforesaid, "so ordered, advised, and commanded the same to be administered," with intent of him to cause her to miscarry, and in order that he might cause the destruction of the life of the child; and that she by means of said ergot, so ordered, advised, and commanded to be administered to her, and so provided by him for her to swallow, and so swallowed, the same thereafter being administered to her by the other defendants with intent of them to cause her to miscarry, and in order that the three defendants might cause the destruction of the life of the child; and that she "by means of said ergot so administered and so provided by" him for her to swallow, and so swallowed, the same having been administered to her by the other defendants in pursuance of his aforesaid order, command, and advice, by him given to them, died, — charges him with administering the ergot as principal, and not as accessory.[1]

[1] Commonwealth *v.* Brown, 14 Gray, 419 (1860).

Indictment against the principal for using an instrument to procure miscarriage, and against an accessory before the fact.[1]

The jurors etc., upon their oath present, that C. D. late of B. in the county of S., physician, on the first day of June in the year of our Lord ——, at B. aforesaid, in the county aforesaid, feloniously, unlawfully, maliciously and without lawful justification, did use a certain instrument, the name of which instrument is to the jurors aforesaid unknown, which instrument the said C. D. in his right hand then and there had and held, by then and there forcing and thrusting the instrument aforesaid, into the body and womb of a certain woman whose name is E. F., the said E. F. being then and there pregnant with child, with intent thereby then and there to cause and procure the miscarriage of the said E. F.; against the peace of said Commonwealth and contrary to the form of the statute in such case made and provided. And the jurors aforesaid, upon their oath aforesaid, do further present, that G. H. late of B. aforesaid, in the county aforesaid, gentleman, before the said felony was committed in manner and form aforesaid, to wit, on the first day of June in the year of our Lord ——, at B. aforesaid, in the county aforesaid, did feloniously and maliciously incite, move, procure, aid, counsel, hire and command the said C. D. the said felony in manner and form aforesaid to do and commit; against the peace of said Commonwealth and contrary to the form of the statute in such case made and provided.

1 See Regina *v.* Ashmall, 9 C. & P. 236 (1840).

CHAPTER IV.

INDICTMENT.

THE crime of abortion, as attempted, or as actually perpetrated, is defined and punished by statutes in England, and in many of the United States. But there is no uniformity in the language of the statutes in either country. The pleader, by attentively considering the operative words of the different statutes, and the decisions of the courts upon them, will have very little difficulty in determining the law applicable to any particular case.

In Pennsylvania, an indictment at common law charged as follows:[1]—

"The Grand Inquest etc. present that J. G. M. of the county aforesaid, dentist, on the tenth day of May in the year of our Lord ——, and on divers other days and times between that day and the taking of this inquisition, in the county aforesaid, and within the jurisdiction of this court, with force and arms, wilfully, maliciously, unlawfully, and wickedly, did administer to and cause to be administered to, and taken by one Mary Elizabeth Lutz, single woman, she the said Mary Elizabeth Lutz, being then and there big and pregnant with child, divers large quantities of deadly, dangerous, unwholesome and pernicious pills, herbs, drugs, potions, teas, liquids, powders, and mixtures; with intent thereby then and there, to cause and procure the miscarriage and abortion of the said child of which the said Mary Elizabeth Lutz was then and there big and pregnant: to the great damage, etc." COULTER J.: "The error assigned is, that the indictment charges the defendant with intent to cause

[1] Mills *v.* Commonwealth, 13 Penn. State Rep. 631 (1850).

and procure the miscarriage and abortion of Mary Elizabeth Lutz, instead of charging the intent to cause and procure the miscarriage and abortion of the child. But it is a misconception of the learned counsel that no abortion can be predicated of the act of untimely birth by foul means. Miscarriage, both by law and philology, means the bringing forth the fœtus before it is perfectly formed and capable of living; and is rightfully predicated of the woman because it refers to the act of premature delivery. The word 'abortion' is synonymous and equivalent to miscarriage in its primary meaning. It has a secondary meaning, in which it is used to denote the offspring. But it was not used in that sense here, and ought not to have been. It is a flagrant crime at common law, to attempt to procure the miscarriage or abortion of the woman, because it interferes with, and violates the mysteries of nature in that process by which the human race is propagated and continued. It is a crime against nature which obstructs the fountain of life, and therefore it is punished."

In Pennsylvania, it was decided, that where the quickness of the woman is alleged in some counts of an indictment, at common law, but is omitted in others; but it is alleged in all of them that the woman is big and pregnant with child, and there is a general verdict of guilty, — there is no error in the record.[1]

Where the language of a statute is general, "to procure the miscarriage of any woman," it is immaterial whether the woman was or was not pregnant at the time.[2] It is therefore unnecessary to allege in an indictment that the woman was "then and there pregnant with child." The earlier English statutes[3] made an important distinction between the case where the woman was quick with child, and

1 Mills v. Commonwealth, 13 Penn. State Rep. 634 (1850).

2 Regina v. Goodhall, 1 Denison C. C. 187, same case as Regina v. Goodchild, 2 C. & K. 293 (1846).

3 43 Geo. III. ch. 58, and 9 Geo. IV. ch. 31, § 14. Ante, pp. 164, 166.

where she was not, or was not proved to be, quick with child; and so clearly showed, that, to constitute an offence within those acts, the woman must have been pregnant at the time.[1]

If there is any doubt as to the drug administered, charge it, in different ways, in several counts, and add a count alleging it to be "a certain noxious thing to the jurors aforesaid unknown."[2]

It is a principle in the law of criminal pleading, that, when a statute makes two or more distinct acts, connected with the same transaction, indictable, each one of which may be considered as representing a stage in the same offence, those which are actually done in the course and progress of its commission may be coupled in one count. On this principle, an indictment, on a statute which inhibits the use of "any means whatever," which charges one of the defendants with using instruments, and the same defendant, with other defendants, with administering drugs to procure a miscarriage, and that by both of said means the woman died, is not bad for duplicity; and proof of the use of either one of the means alleged is sufficient to warrant a conviction.[3]

A statute prohibits the use of "any means whatever" to procure miscarriage. It also provides, that if the woman shall die in consequence of the doing of any of the acts prohibited, which are done to procure and cause her miscarriage, the punishment to be inflicted upon the offender shall, to a certain specified extent, be increased and aggravated. An indictment which avers that the defendant, by one or more of the means described in the statute, with the intent to procure her miscarriage, killed the woman, is only alleging in another form of words, that she died in consequence thereof, and does not charge the crime of manslaughter.[4]

[1] Rex *v.* Scudder, 1 Moody C. C. 216, and 3 C. & P. 605 (1829).

[2] Archbold Crim. Pl. (London ed. 1853), 518.

[3] Commonwealth *v.* Brown, 14 Gray, 419 (1860).

[4] Commonwealth *v.* Brown, 14 Gray, 419 (1860).

An indictment which charges the use of instruments, the administering of drugs, and the thrusting the hand into the womb after the coming forth of the child, and the death of the woman in consequence of all the means so used, the averment of violence by the hand of the defendant at that period, constitutes no part of the description of the acts prohibited by the statute, and is therefore an immaterial and superfluous statement, and may well be rejected as surplusage.[1]

In New York, by statute, Laws of 1845, ch. 260, § 2, it is a misdemeanor to administer drugs, etc., to any pregnant woman *with intent to procure a miscarriage;* and by statute, Laws of 1846, ch. 22, § 1, it is manslaughter (a felony) to use the same means, *with intent to destroy the child,* in case the death of the child is thereby produced. An indictment charged all the facts necessary to constitute the crime of manslaughter, except the intent with which the acts were done; and, in conclusion, alleged that the accused "did feloniously and wilfully kill and slay" the child. The intent averred was an *intent to produce a miscarriage.* It was decided, on error, that the indictment was fatally defective for the felony, but [sufficient] to sustain a conviction for the misdemeanor.[2]

In Indiana, the language of the statute is, "Every person who shall wilfully administer to any pregnant woman any medicine, drug, substance, or thing whatever, or employ any instrument, etc., with intent to procure the miscarriage of any woman," etc. An indictment charged that the defendant at a certain time and place "did feloniously, wilfully, and unlawfully administer to one L. H., then and there being pregnant with a child, a large quantity of medicine, with intent thereby feloniously, etc., to procure the miscarriage of said L. H., the administering said medi-

[1] Commonwealth *v.* Brown, 14 Gray, 419 (1860).

[2] Lohman *v.* The People, 1 Comstock, 379 (1848), affirming, s.c. 2 Barbour, 216; followed in People *v.* Stockham, 1 Parker, 424 (1853).

cine to said L. H. not then and there being necessary to preserve the life of said L. H., contrary to the statute," etc. The objection to the indictment was, that it neither named the medicine administered, nor alleged that it was noxious. BLACKFORD J.: "This statute, so far as the present case is concerned, is similar to the second section of the statute, 43 Geo. III. ch. 58; and it has been held, that, on the trial of an indictment on that section, the name of the medicine administered need not be proved; that the question is, whether the prisoner administered any matter or thing to the woman with intent to procure abortion.[1] If the name of the medicine need not be proved, there seems to be no good reason for naming it in the indictment. It is also decided, in the case just referred to, that the indictment need not describe the medicine as noxious."[2]

In Massachusetts, the statute 1845, ch. 27, enacts, that "Whoever, maliciously, or without lawful justification, with intent to cause and procure the miscarriage of a woman then pregnant with child, shall administer to her, prescribe for her, or advise or direct her to take or swallow, any poison, drug, medicine, or noxious thing, or shall cause or procure her with like intent, to take or swallow any poison, drug, medicine, or noxious thing; and whoever maliciously, and without lawful justification, shall use any instrument or means whatever with the like intent, and every person with the like intent, knowingly aiding and assisting such offender or offenders, shall be deemed guilty of felony, if the woman die in consequence thereof, and shall be imprisoned not more than twenty years, nor less than five years, in the State prison; and if the woman doth not die in consequence thereof, such offender shall be guilty of a misdemeanor, and shall be punished by imprisonment not exceeding seven years, nor less than one year, in the State prison or house of correction or common jail, and by fine not exceeding two thousand dollars."

1 Rex v. Phillips, 3 Campb. 73 (1811).

2 The State v. Vawter, 7 Blackford, 592 (1845).

An indictment on this statute need not allege that the child with which the woman was pregnant was alive, or that she was quick with child; nor whether she died or not in consequence of the operation.[1] Nor is it necessary to prove that she was quick with child. The statute was intended to supply the supposed defects of the common law, and applies to all cases of pregnancy.[2] The indictment in *Commonwealth* v. *Wood*,[3] which was drawn on this statute, averred that the defendant at a certain time and place, "maliciously and without lawful justification, did force and thrust a certain metallic instrument, which the said Wood then and there had and held in his hand, into the womb and body of a certain woman by the name of Sarah Chaffee, the said Sarah being then and there pregnant with child, with the wicked and unlawful intent of the said Wood then and there thereby to cause and procure the said Sarah to miscarry and prematurely to bring forth the said child with which she was then and there pregnant as aforesaid and the said Sarah at said place and time, by means of the said forcing and thrusting of said instrument into the womb and body of the said Sarah in manner aforesaid, did bring forth said child, of which she was so pregnant, dead; against the peace," etc. This count was held not to be open to objection, as not alleging that the defendant used the instrument, nor who the woman was nor what was her name, nor that she brought forth the child prematurely, nor brought it forth dead in consequence of what the defendant had done.

The General Statutes of Massachusetts, ch. 165, § 9, enact: —

"Whoever, with intent to procure miscarriage of any woman, unlawfully administers to her, or advises or prescribes for her, or causes to be taken by her, any poison, drug, medicine, or other noxious thing, or unlawfully uses any instrument or other means whatever with the like intent,

1 Larned *v.* Commonwealth, 12 Met. 241 (1847).

2 Commonwealth *v.* Wood, 11 Gray, 86 (1858).

3 11 Gray, 86 (1858).

or with like intent aids or assists therein, shall, if the woman dies in consequence thereof, be imprisoned in the State prison not exceeding twenty, nor less than five years, and if the woman does not die in consequence thereof, shall be punished by imprisonment in the State prison not exceeding seven years, nor less than one year, and by fine not exceeding two thousand dollars."

In *Commonwealth* v. *Sholes*,[1] an indictment which was drawn under this statute alleged that the defendant, at a certain time and place, "unlawfully did use a certain instrument," in a manner which was particularly described, in and upon a certain woman who was pregnant, "with intent then and thereby to cause and procure the miscarriage of said woman." It was held, that the indictment need not allege that the act was done "maliciously and without lawful justification:" it is sufficient to allege that it was unlawfully done, with intent to cause and procure the miscarriage.[2] GRAY J.: "An objection taken to the indictment is, that the defendant is not alleged to have committed the act therein described 'maliciously and without lawful justification.' But we are of opinion that no such allegation was necessary. The indictment following the words of the Gen. Sts. ch. 165, § 9, on which it is based, alleges that

[1] 13 Allen, 554 (1866).

[2] The defendant's counsel argued thus: —

I. *Maliciously.* The indictment charges, that the defendant "unlawfully" did, etc. All his acts may have been "unlawful," and yet no crime have been committed. "A mere guilty intention is not sufficient to constitute a crime. There must be an intent coupled with an overt act tending to the perpetration of the crime." POLLOCK C. B., in Regina *v.* Isaacs, Leigh & Cave C. C. 224. Legal malice is defined in Commonwealth *v.* York, 9 Met. 105, as "a wrongful act done intentionally, without just cause or excuse." The word "unlawfully" does not embrace all this. It has no technical meaning; and, although it is in the statute on which this indictment was founded, and the omission of it would vitiate the indictment, still this is not one of the class of cases in which, in describing an offence, it is sufficient to pursue the very words of the statute. HAWKINS P.C. bk. 2, ch. 25, § 111. The word "maliciously" imports a criminal motive, intent, or purpose. Commonwealth *v.* Walden, 3 Cush. 558.

II. *Without lawful justification.* Where the potion is given, or other means

the defendant did the act described, 'unlawfully,' and 'with intent to cause and procure the miscarriage of the said woman,' and sufficiently sets forth a criminal act and a criminal intent. The word 'unlawfully' negatives and precludes any inference or possibility that the act was done by a surgeon for the purpose of saving the life of the woman, or under any other circumstances which would furnish a lawful justification. Any unlawful use of an instrument, with intent to procure miscarriage, is made criminal by the statute. The learned counsel for the defendant admit, that, if the word 'feloniously' had been inserted in the indictment, their objection could not be supported; and the Gen. Sts. ch. 168, § 2, provide that 'it shall not be necessary to allege in any indictment or complaint that the offence charged is a felony, or felonious, or done feloniously; nor shall any indictment or complaint be quashed or deemed invalid by reason of the omission of the words 'felony,' 'felonious,' or 'feloniously.'"[1]

Indictment for administering a certain noxious thing with intent to procure miscarriage. — Gen. Sts. of Mass. ch. 165, § 9.

The jurors, etc., upon their oath present, that C. D. late of B. in the county of S. gentleman, on the first day of June in the year of our Lord ——, at B. aforesaid in the county aforesaid, feloniously and unlawfully did administer to a certain woman whose name is E. F., a large quantity,

of causing abortion.are used, by a surgeon, for the purpose of saving the life of a woman, the case is free from malice, and has a lawful justification. Report of the Mass. Crim. Law Commissioners in 1844, title "Abortion." I. note *a*. The operative words of the English statute, 7 Will. IV. and 1 Vict. ch. 85, § 6, are like those of the General Statutes. And all the precedents charge that the defendant "*feloniously* and unlawfully," did, etc. ARCHBOLD Crim. Pl. 14th London ed. p. 551, and 4th Am. ed. p. 414. ARCHBOLD'S Consolidated Statutes, p. 115. Precedent in Appendix to 6 Cox C. C. p. xcix. If the word "feloniously" had been inserted in this indictment, the objection, that the crime should have been alleged to have been committed "maliciously and without justification," could not be supported. That word would sufficiently show the *intent* with which the act was committed. DENMAN, arguendo in The King *v.* Towle, 2 Marshall, 468.

1 Commonwealth *v.* Jackson, 15 Gray, 187.

to wit, two ounces of a certain noxious thing, called savin, with intent thereby then and there to cause and procure the miscarriage of the said E. F. [*If the woman die in consequence, proceed as follows:* —][1] And the jurors aforesaid, upon their oath aforesaid, do further present, that the said E. F., afterwards, to wit, on the first day of July in the year of our Lord ——, at B. aforesaid, in the county aforesaid, by means of the noxious thing aforesaid, so as aforesaid, in manner and form aforesaid administered by the said C. D., and taken and swallowed by the said E. F., then and there died; against the peace etc.

Indictment for using instruments with intent to procure miscarriage. — Gen. Sts. of Mass. ch. 165, § 9.

The jurors etc., upon their oath present, that C. D. late of B. in the county of S. physician, on the first day of June in the year of our Lord ——, at B. aforesaid in the county aforesaid, feloniously and unlawfully did use a certain instrument, the name of which instrument is to the jurors aforesaid unknown, which instrument the said C. D. in his right hand then and there had and held, by then and there forcing and thrusting the instrument aforesaid, into the body and womb of a certain woman whose name is E. F., with intent thereby then and there to cause and procure the miscarriage of the said E. F.; against the peace of said Commonwealth and contrary to the form of the statute in such case made and provided.

The General Statutes of Massachusetts, ch. 165, § 10, enact: —

"Whoever knowingly advertises, prints, publishes, distributes, or circulates, or knowingly causes to be advertised, printed, published, distributed, or circulated, any pamphlet, printed paper, book, newspaper, notice, advertisement, or reference, containing words or language giving or conveying any notice, hint or reference, to any person, or to the name of any person, real or fictitious, from whom, or to any place,

[1] But it is unnecessary. Commonwealth *v.* Wood, 11 Gray, 86 (1858).

house, shop, or office, where, any poison, drug, mixture, preparation, medicine, or noxious thing, or any instrument or means whatever, or any advice, direction, information, or knowledge, may be obtained for the purpose of causing or procuring the miscarriage of any woman pregnant with child, shall be punished by imprisonment in the State prison or jail not exceeding three years, or by fine not exceeding one thousand dollars."

Indictment for circulating an advertisement relative to procuring miscarriage. — Gen. Sts. of Mass. ch. 165, § 10.[1]

The jurors etc., upon their oath present, that C. D. late of B. in the county of S., physician, on the first day of June in the year of our Lord ——, at B. aforesaid, in the county aforesaid, feloniously, unlawfully and knowingly did publish, distribute, and circulate [*or*, unlawfully and knowingly did cause to be published, distributed, and circulated] a certain advertisement, containing words and language giving and conveying notice, hint, and reference to a certain place where a medicine, advice, direction, knowledge and information may be obtained, for the purpose of causing and procuring the miscarriage of any woman pregnant with child, which advertisement, published, circulated, and distributed as aforesaid, is of the tenor following, that is to say [*here set out an exact copy of the advertisement*]; against the peace of said Commonwealth, and contrary to the form of the statute in such case made and provided.

In Maine, it is enacted, that "Every person, who shall use and employ any instrument with intent to destroy the child of which a woman may be pregnant, whether such child be quick or not, and shall thereupon destroy such child before its birth, shall be punished by imprisonment in the State prison, not more than five years, or by fine," etc. Rev. Sts. ch. 160, § 13. "The offence described in this section,"

[1] In an indictment under this statute, it is advisable to insert different counts, charging the offence in different ways.

said TENNEY J.,[1] "is not committed unless the act be done with an intent to destroy such child as is there referred to, and it be destroyed by the means used for the purpose. It is required by established rules of criminal pleading, that the intention, which prompted the act that caused the destruction of the child, as well as the act itself, and the death of the child thereby produced, should be fully set out in the indictment, in order to constitute a crime punishable by imprisonment in the State prison, under the statute. The allegation, that a certain instrument was used upon a woman pregnant, and that the use of that instrument caused her to bring forth the child dead, is not a charge, that the one using the instrument intended to destroy the child. The inference of such design, from the use of the instrument, and its effect, is by no means necessary. The third count in the indictment alleges the act to have been done with the intent to cause and procure the deceased to *miscarry* and *bring forth* the child of which she was then pregnant and quick, and that by means of that act, she brought forth the child dead. But there is no allegation, that the act was done with the *intention* that she should bring forth her child dead, or with an intent to destroy it, unless the words *miscarry*, and *bring forth the child*, necessarily include its destruction. The expulsion of the ovum or embryo, within the first six weeks after conception, is technically *miscarriage;* between that time and the expiration of the sixth month, when the child may by possibility live, it is termed abortion; if the delivery be soon after the sixth month, it is termed premature labor. But the criminal attempt to destroy the fœtus, at any time before birth, is termed in law a *miscarriage*, varying, as we have seen, in degree of offence and punishment, whether the attempt were before or after the child had quickened.[2] Other writers on the subject give a similar definition of the term 'mis-

[1] Smith *v.* The State, 32 Maine, 48, 58 (1851).

[2] CHITTY's Med. Jurisp. 410.

carriage.'[1] The converse of this last proposition cannot be true, as there are undoubtedly many miscarriages, involving no moral wrong. If the term *miscarriage* were to be understood in the indictment, in its most limited sense, it cannot be denied, that, in effect, it must be identical with the destruction of the fœtus. But this indictment itself has given to the word 'miscarriage' the more general signification. It charges, that the miscarriage was of the woman who was pregnant, and 'quick with child.' The term 'quick with child' is a term known to the law, and courts are presumed to understand its meaning. A woman cannot be 'quick with child' until a period much later than six weeks from the commencement of the term of gestation. The more general meaning of the word miscarriage must therefore be applied. The indictment charges no time, after the quickening, when the miscarriage took place. It may have been at any period when the birth would have been premature. The language of the indictment, when taken together, construed in its ordinary or in its technical and legal signification,[2] does not forbid this. And labor is premature, if it take place at any period before the completion of the natural time. It is admitted by Dr. PARIS, a writer of high repute on Medical Jurisprudence, from the number of established cases, it is possible that the fœtus may survive, and be reared to maturity, though born at very early periods. Many ancient instances are stated of births even at four months and a half, with continued life even till the age of twenty-four years. And the Parliament of Paris decreed, that an infant at five months possessed the capability of

[1] HOBLYN'S Dictionary of Terms used in Medicine and other Collateral Sciences.

[2] It is a clear principle, that the language of an indictment must be construed by the rules of pleading, and not by the common interpretation put on ordinary language; for nothing indeed differs more widely in construction than the same matter when viewed by the rules of pleading, and when construed by the language of ordinary life. ERLE J., in Regina *v.* Thompson, 4 Eng. Law & Eq. Rep. 292.

living to the ordinary period of human existence; and it has been asserted, that a child delivered at the age only of five months and eight days may live; or, according to BECK and others, if born at six months after conception.[1] Many of the facts upon which the opinions of writers upon medical jurisprudence are founded, may be erroneous, and the opinions incorrect. We cannot take judicial notice of either. But it is not too much to say, that a child may be born living, when its birth may be so soon after conception, that it is premature. The fœtus may be expelled, by unlawful means, so soon after conception, that extra-uterine life cannot continue for any considerable length of time, and yet after birth it may once exercise all the functions of a living child. We have found no authority that this may not be termed a miscarriage, if the word is not confined to its most limited meaning; and, if it be so, it is not perceived that it ceases to be correct, if the life of the child prematurely born is further prolonged. It is quite clear, therefore, that the word *miscarriage* in its legal acceptation, and as used in this indictment, does not necessarily include the destruction of the child before its birth; and a design to cause its *miscarriage* is not the same thing as a design to *destroy* the child. The other term used in the indictment, 'to bring forth the said child,' does not imply even a premature birth. Consequently it gives no additional strength to the charge."

[1] CHITTY's Med. Jurisp. 410, 411.

CHAPTER V.

EVIDENCE.

1. *An Infusion or Decoction of a Shrub are* ejusdem generis. *The Question upon* 43 *Geo.* III. *ch.* 58, § 2, *was, whether any Matter or Thing was administered to procure Abortion.*

An indictment upon the 43 Geo. III. ch. 58, § 2, charged the prisoner with having administered to a woman a *decoction* of a certain shrub called *savin:* and it appeared upon the evidence, that the prisoner prepared the medicine which he administered, by pouring boiling water on the leaves of a shrub. The medical men who were examined stated, that such a preparation is called an *infusion*, and not a *decoction* (which is made by boiling the substance in the water); upon which the prisoner's counsel insisted that he was entitled to an acquittal, on the ground that the medicine was misdescribed. But Lawrence J. overruled the objection, and said, that infusion and decoction are *ejusdem generis*, and that the variance was immaterial: that the question was, whether the prisoner administered any matter or thing to the woman to procure abortion.[1]

[1] Rex *v.* Phillips, 3 Campb. 74 (1811). The State *v.* Vawter, 7 Blackford, 592 (1845). And in Rex *v.* Coe, 6 C. & P. 403 (1834), where the prisoner was indicted on the 9 Geo. IV. ch. 31, § 13, for administering saffron to a female, and his counsel was cross-examining as to her having taken something else before the saffron, and also as to the innoxious nature of the article, —

2. *Noxious Thing.*

On an indictment for administering featherfew and other drugs to procure abortion, it appeared that the prisoner gave the woman, who was alleged to be with child by him, two powders, with directions to take one on each of two successive nights, and said that the effect would be to cause miscarriage. She took one of the powders, with the featherfew, which brought on violent sickness. The other powder was examined by a physician, and he could not discover any mineral substance in it; as far as he could judge from the taste, smell, and appearance, it was a mixture of savin and fennigreek, the latter being the larger ingredient. The fennigreek would scarcely produce any effect at all; savin, in that quantity, might produce a little disturbance in the stomach for the time, but would do no further injury. Featherfew[1] is an herb very similar to camomile: it is a tonic in common use among the peasantry, and has nothing noxious in it. A mixture of the powder and decoction of this herb would not alter the properties of either. The prisoner upon two or three subsequent occasions had brought

VAUGHAN B. said: "Does that signify? It is with the intention, that the jury have to do; and if the prisoner administered a bit of bread merely, with intent to procure abortion, it is sufficient." It is not stated upon which branch of the section this indictment was framed; if upon the latter, which used the words 'any medicine or other thing,' perhaps the dictum was right. But it should seem that neither this dictum nor that of LAWRENCE J. in Rex *v.* Phillips, apply to the new statute, 24 & 25 Vict. ch. 100, § 58, which uses the words 'any poison or other noxious thing,' only in the case of administering or causing to be taken; and although a doubt has been suggested in a note to Rex *v.* Coe, as to whether the words 'other means' might not be applied to other substances than such as are poisonous or noxious, it should seem that the words 'other means' cannot be so applied in the new act; first, because they are in an entirely distinct sentence; secondly, because they are governed by the word 'use,' and not by 'administer.'" Note by Mr. GREAVES, RUSSELL on Crimes, I. 901.

[1] The proper name of this is feverfew, matricaria, so called from its supposed use in disorders of the womb. Edinb. Med. & Phys. Dict.

the woman other medicines to take for the same purpose, some of which she had taken, but not the rest. WILDE C.J. held, that the evidence was not sufficient to prove that the drugs administered came within the meaning of the words "poison or other noxious thing."[1]

As the prisoner administered the drugs with intent to procure a miscarriage, and as savin is unquestionably in its nature a noxious drug, the decision in this case seems open to great doubt. It is submitted that the true meaning of the words "poison or other noxious thing" is such things as in their nature are poisonous or noxious; and that it is a misapprehension to suppose that the statute requires such a quantity of a poison or other noxious thing to be administered as shall be noxious. If a person administers any quantity of a poison, however small, it has never yet been doubted, that, if it were done with intent to murder, the offence of administering poison with intent to murder was complete; and *Regina* v. *Cluderay*,[2] which was decided after this case, shows that if poison be administered in such a way that it cannot injure, the offence is nevertheless complete; and WILDE C.J. there said, "The act of administering poison with intent to kill, is proved. *The effect of that act is beside the question.*" It is submitted, therefore, that, if there be an intent to procure abortion, it is quite immaterial how small the quantity be of the poison or other noxious thing that is administered.[3]

It was held, on the 43 Geo. III. ch. 58, § 2, that, unless the woman were with child, the offence was not committed, although the prisoner thought she was with child, and administered the drug with intent to destroy the child.[4] But the new act, 24 & 25 Vict. ch. 100, makes this immaterial, except in cases where the mother is the offender.

1 Regina *v.* Perry, 2 Cox C. C. 223 (1847).
2 1 Denison C. C. 514 (1849).
3 Note by Mr. GREAVES, RUSSELL on Crimes, I. 902.
4 Rex *v.* Scudder, 1 Moody C. C. 216, and 3 C. & P. 605 (1828).

3. *What is an Administering and Causing to be Taken.*

To constitute an administering, or causing to be taken, it is not necessary that there should be a delivery by the hand. If a person mix poison with coffee, and tell another that the coffee is for her, and she take it in consequence, it seems that this is an administering; and, at all events, it is a causing the poison to be taken. Upon an indictment under the 9 Geo. IV. ch. 31, § 11, some counts of which charged that the prisoner "administered," and others, that she "caused to be taken," poison, with intent to murder, etc., it appeared that a coffee-pot, which was proved to contain arsenic mixed with coffee, was standing by the side of the grate: the prosecutrix was going to pour out some tea, but on the prisoner telling her that the coffee was for her, she poured out some for herself, and drank it, and in about five minutes became very ill. It was objected, that the mere mixing of poison, and leaving it in some place for the person to take it, was not sufficient to constitute an administering; and *Rex* v. *Cadman*[1] was relied on, as showing that the delivery of the poison by the hand of the prisoner is the main ingredient of the offence; that there was no count which did not require an agency on the part of the prisoner. A "causing to be taken" included an act, and so did an "attempt to administer." PARK J. (in summing up): "There has been much argument whether, in this case, there has been an administering of this poison. It has been contended that there must be a manual delivery of the poison, and the law, as stated in RYAN & MOODY's Reports, goes that way; but as my notes differ from that report, and also from my own feelings, I am inclined to think that some error has crept into that report. It is there stated that the judges thought swallowing of the poison not essential; but my recollection is, that the judges held just

[1] 1 Moody C. C. 114. See the next page.

the contrary. I am inclined to hold that there was an administering here; and I am of opinion that, to constitute an administering, it is not necessary that there should be a delivery by the hand. With respect to the question, whether the prisoner 'did cause the poison to be taken' by Mrs. S., it has been proved that she said that she put the coffee-pot down for Mrs. S., and that upon this Mrs. S. drank some of the coffee; and if you believe the evidence of Mrs. S., I am of opinion that this is a 'causing to be taken,' within the Act of Parliament."[1]

To constitute an administering, or causing to be taken, a mere delivery to the woman is not sufficient: the poison must be taken into the mouth, and, it seems, some of it must have been actually swallowed. The prisoner was indicted under the 43 Geo. III. ch. 58, for administering white arsenic and sulphate of copper, with intent to murder. It appeared that the prisoner pulled a white-bread cake out of his pocket, and pinched off a bit from the outside of it, and gave it the prosecutrix to eat, and she took it and put it into her mouth, but spit it out again, and did not swallow any part of it; it was proved that the cake contained arsenic and sulphate of copper: it was objected that it ought to be proved that the poison was swallowed by, or taken into the stomach of, the person intended to be poisoned; and upon a case reserved, the judges seemed to think swallowing not essential; but they were of opinion that a mere delivery to the woman did not constitute an administering; and that, upon a statute so highly penal, they ought not to go beyond what was meant by the word "administering;" and a pardon was therefore recommended.[2]

[1] Rex *v.* Harley, 4 C. & P. 369 (1830).

[2] Rex *v.* Cadman, 1 Moody C. C. 114 (1825). But in Carrington's Supplement, 237, where the same case is reported, it is stated, that the judges held, that it was not an administering, unless the poison was taken into the stomach; and in Rex *v.* Harley, 4 C. & P. 371 (1830), PARK J. in the course of the trial, said, that his note of this case was, "that the judges were unanimously of opinion that the poison had not been administered, because it had

In *Regina* v. *Wilson*,[1] the prisoner was convicted on an indictment for "unlawfully administering to, and causing to be taken" by, one Emma Cheney certain poison (in the second count stated to be a certain noxious thing), with intent to procure her miscarriage. It appeared that she, being and believing herself to be pregnant, applied to the prisoner to get her something to procure her miscarriage, and that the prisoner accordingly purchased some preparation of mercury, which he gave to her, directing her to take one-half of the quantity in gin. Cheney accordingly procured the gin, and, in the absence of the prisoner, took the dose, which produced a miscarriage. The jury found these facts, and that the mercury was both given by the prisoner to Cheney and taken by her with intent to procure the miscarriage; and, upon a case reserved, it was held, that the prisoner was properly convicted, as there was a "causing to be taken" within the meaning of the statute. Cheney, though culpable, was not guilty of felony, and therefore not guilty of the felony created by the statute; and the prisoner was therefore the only person coming within the words as principal; and this distinguishes the case from *Regina* v. *Williams*.[2] So where, on a similar indictment, it appeared that the prisoner had talked with L. Chuter about her being with child, and brought her a bunch of savin, and told her, if she put it in some gin, and took from half a glass to a glass two or three times a week, it would destroy her child; and she took the savin and gin three or four times accordingly; and the prisoner afterwards induced Chuter to get some blue pills from a chemist, which the prisoner made up with some

not been taken into the stomach, but only into the mouth;" and this certainly is confirmed by the fact that a pardon was recommended; which would be correct, according to this view of the decision; but incorrect, if it was sufficient to prove, that the poison was taken into the mouth, as that was proved to have been done. Note by Mr. GREAVES, RUSSELL on Crimes, I. 988.

[1] Dearsly & Bell C. C. 127; 7 Cox C. C. 190; 2 Jur. N.S. 1146 (1856).

[2] 1 Denison C. C. 39 (1844).

flour and tea into pills, of which Chuter took twenty or thirty, and was very ill from the time of taking the pills till she was confined, — it was held, upon a case reserved, that there was no distinction between this and the preceding case, *Regina* v. *Wilson*.[1] It is not stated expressly whether the savin and pills were taken in the absence of the prisoner; but the inference from the facts stated is that they were.[2]

It is to be observed, that, under the statute 24 & 25 Vict. ch. 100, in such cases as the two last, the woman being with child would be a principal, and the man an accessory before the fact; but where the woman is not with child, these cases will still apply; for then the woman's criminality will be exactly the same as it was under the former act.[3]

In New Jersey, the language of a statute approved in 1849 is, "If any person or persons, maliciously or without lawful justification, with intent to cause and procure the miscarriage of a woman then pregnant with child, shall administer to her, prescribe for her, or advise or direct her to take or swallow any poison, drug, medicine, or noxious thing," such offender shall, etc. It is a crime within the meaning of this statute to advise, without lawful justification, a pregnant woman to take some noxious thing with intent to cause her miscarriage. The actual taking or swallowing of the drug constitutes no element of the crime. The defendant's guilt is complete by giving the advice with the intent specified in the statute, and it is immaterial whether the advice is followed or not. Advising to take the potion is the overt act made criminal by the statute. "The design of the statute," said the Chief Justice, in delivering the opinion of the court, "was not to prevent the procuring of abortions so much as to guard the health and life of the mother against the consequences of such attempts. The

[1] Regina *v.* Farrow, Dearsly & Bell C. C. 164; 3 Jur. N.S. 167; 28 L. T. Rep. 311 (1857).

[2] See also Regina *v.* Gaylor, Dearsly & Bell C. C. 127; 7 Cox C. C. (1856), ante, p. 173.

[3] Russell on Crimes, I. 902.

guilt of the defendant is not graduated by the success or failure of the attempt. It is immaterial whether the fœtus is destroyed, or whether it has quickened or not. In either case the degree of the defendant's guilt is the same."[1]

4. *Procuring Drugs, etc., to cause Abortion.*

In a very recent case it was decided, that, in order to constitute the offence of supplying a noxious substance, with the intention that it shall be employed in procuring abortion within the meaning of the fifty-ninth section 24 & 25 Vict. ch. 100, it is not necessary that the intention of employing it should exist in the mind of any other person than the person supplying it.[2] Upon the trial, it was contended by the counsel for the defendant, that there was no case against him, because, among other objections, it was necessary that the defendant should know that the poison or noxious thing is intended to be unlawfully used or employed with intent to procure the miscarriage of any woman; whereas it was not intended, except by the defendant himself, to be so used at all. The jury found, that the woman did not intend to take the substance in question, nor did any other person, except only the defendant himself, intend that she should take it. The jury found a verdict of guilty, and the presiding judge reserved the case. ERLE C.J.: "The question asked of us is, whether the intention of any other person than the defendant is necessary to the commission of the offence made punishable under this statute. We are all of opinion, that that question should be answered in the negative. The statute is directed against the supplying of any substance, with the intention that it shall be employed in procuring abortion. The prisoner supplied the substance, and intended that it should be employed to procure abor-

1 The State v. Murphy, 3 Dutcher, 112 (1858).

2 Regina v. Hillman, Leigh & Cave C. C. 343; 9 Cox C. C. 386; 9 L. T. Rep. N.S. 518 (1863).

tion. He knew of his own intention that it should be so employed; and is, therefore, within the words of the statute, as we construe them. He is also, in our opinion, within the mischief of the statute, and ought to be convicted. That is the question for us, and that is our answer."

Upon the trial of an indictment under the fifty-ninth section of the statute 24 & 25 Vict. ch. 100, it is necessary to prove that the thing supplied is noxious. The supplying an innoxious drug, whatever may be the intent of the person supplying it, is not an offence within the meaning of the statute.[1] POLLOCK C.B.: "A mere guilty intention is not sufficient to constitute a crime. There must be an intent, coupled with an overt act tending to the perpetration of the crime.[2] The administration of pure water is no offence within the section under which this woman was indicted." In this case, the surgeon testified, that a thing, otherwise of a perfectly harmless character, may be noxious by exciting the imagination of the woman, and thereby producing abortion. But the case clearly decides that it is not sufficient that the defendant merely imagined that the thing administered would have the effect intended; but it must appear that the drug administered was either a "poison" or "noxious thing."

5. *In General.*

On an indictment for administering savin with intent to procure abortion, the administration of savin on one day was proved, and it was proposed on the part of the prosecution to prove the administration of similar drugs on many subsequent days, for the purpose of showing the intent, and also as part of the same felony; and it was urged that the

1 Regina *v.* Isaacs, Leigh & Cave C. C. 220; 9 Cox C. C. 228; 9 Jur. N.S. 212; 7 L. T. Rep. N.S. 365 (1862).

2 The law will not take notice of an intent without an act. Regina *v.* Eagleton, Dearsly C. C. 538. Regina *v.* Roberts, Dearsly C. C. 551, per PARKE B.

substance of the felony was the administration of drugs for the purpose of procuring abortion, and if that were done by homœopathic doses, taken for a long period, all would form part of one felony; but CRESSWELL J. held, that other matters of the same description might be proved for the purpose of showing the intent, but that the administration of other savin on other days could not be given in evidence as part of the offence.[1] On the trial of an indictment for administering featherfew and other drugs to procure abortion, it appeared that the prisoner gave the woman, who was alleged to be with child by him, two powders, with directions to take one on each of two successive nights, *and said that the effect would be to cause miscarriage.* The prisoner, upon two or three subsequent occasions, had brought the woman other medicines to take for the same purpose, some of which she had taken, but not the rest. WILDE C.J. held, that the other transactions were admissible as showing the intent with which the particular drugs referred to in the indictment were administered.[2] *Sed quære.* "The law of England," said Lord CAMPBELL C.J. "does not allow one crime to be proved in order to raise a probability that another crime has been committed by the perpetrator of the first."[3]

Where the evidence showed that ergot was administered to the deceased shortly before her death, it was held, that it was competent for the prosecution to prove that it was the popular opinion that ergot would produce abortion. "The fact proved might show a motive for administering it, and the intention with which it was done."[4]

In Massachusetts, the St. 1845, ch. 27, enacts, that "Whoever maliciously or without lawful justification, with intent to cause and procure the miscarriage of a woman then preg-

[1] Regina *v.* Calder, 1 Cox C. C. 348 (1844).
[2] Regina *v.* Perry, 2 Cox C. C. 223 (1847). The prisoner was acquitted.
[3] Regina *v.* Oddy, as reported in 4 Eng. Law & Eq. Rep. 574.
[4] Carter *v.* The State, 2 Carter, 617 (1851).

nant with child, shall," etc. Under this statute, the act would seem to be malicious if it had no lawful justification. But it would clearly be malicious if done from any wicked or base motive; and the consent of the woman, or the desire to screen her from exposure or disgrace, is no justification.[1]

On an indictment for procuring a miscarriage, the judge instructed the jury, that the woman was not technically an accomplice, and therefore, strictly speaking, the rule in relation to the corroboration of an accomplice did not apply; but, inasmuch as she in a moral point of view was implicated, it would be proper for the jury to consider that circumstance in its bearing upon her credibility; that it was also their duty to consider all the evidence in the case tending to contradict her, as affecting the credit they would give to her, her credibility being entirely a question for them; and declined to instruct them, that, if she swore falsely upon any material point in the case, it so far discredited her whole testimony that they should not place any reliance upon it. *Held*, that the defendant had no ground of exception.[2]

On an indictment for procuring a miscarriage, the Commonwealth may introduce evidence of the health and spirits of the patient, and of stains and marks upon her bedclothes, a month afterwards.[3]

On an indictment for procuring a miscarriage, after evidence introduced by the defendant that the patient was pregnant some months after the operation is alleged to have been performed, the Commonwealth may prove by her that she had sexual intercourse with the defendant between the times of the alleged operation and of the subsequent pregnancy.[4]

On an indictment for using instruments to procure a miscarriage, thereby causing death, injured parts of the

1 Commonwealth *v.* Wood, 11 Gray, 86 (1858).
2 Commonwealth *v.* Wood, 11 Gray, 85 (1858).
3 Commonwealth *v.* Wood, 11 Gray, (1858).
4 Commonwealth *v.* Wood, 11 Gray, (1858).

body of the deceased woman, preserved in spirits, may be exhibited to the jury in connection with the testimony of the physician who made the post-mortem examination.[1]

The fact of the secretion of a fœtus about the building where the offence is alleged to have been committed, is admissible in evidence as tending to prove the corpus delicti.[2]

On an indictment for advising and procuring one Susanna Guyer, a pregnant woman, to take a certain medicine, with intent to procure her miscarriage, the counsel for the defendant having avowed their intention to insist that one Hodge was the father of the child, and not the defendant, it was decided that it was competent for the government to prove by the testimony of Hodge that he had never had sexual intercourse with Susanna Guyer.[3] "In such a case, the woman does not stand legally in the situation of an accomplice; for, although she no doubt participated in the moral offence imputed to the defendant, she could not have been indicted for that offence. The law regards her rather as the victim than the perpetrator of the crime."

Certain declarations and acts are admitted as original evidence, being distinguished from hearsay by their connection with the principal fact under investigation. Thus, where a person changes his actual residence, or domicile, or leaves his home, or returns thither, or remains abroad, his declarations made at the time of the transaction, and expressive of its character, motive, or object, are regarded as "verbal acts, indicating a present purpose and intention," and are therefore admitted in evidence, like any other material facts.[4] Where the fact, that a person since deceased

[1] Commonwealth *v.* Brown, 14 Gray, 419 (1860).

[2] The State *v.* Howard, 32 Vermont, 405 (1850).

[3] Dunn *v.* The People, 2 Tiffany, 523 (1864).

[4] GREENL. Ev. I. § 108. TAYLOR Ev. I. § 521. PURCELL Crim. Pl. & Ev. 289. This rule was well stated by Chief Justice HOSMER: "Declarations, to become part of the res gestæ, must have been made at the time of the act done, which they are supposed to characterize, and have been well calculated to unfold the nature and quality of the facts they were intended to explain, and so to harmonize with them as obviously to constitute one transaction." Enos *v.* Tuttle, 3 Connecticut, 250.

went to the house of the defendant for the purpose of having him procure an abortion upon her person, was material, it was held, that the declarations of such person, indicating her purpose and intention of going there, made at the time of her departure for his house, were admissible in evidence as part of the res gestæ.[1]

The acts and declarations of one of a company of conspirators, in regard to the common design, are evidence against his fellows. Here a foundation should first be laid by proof, sufficient, in the opinion of the judge, to establish primâ facie the fact of conspiracy between the parties, or, at least, proper to be laid before the jury, as tending to establish such fact. The connection of the individuals in the unlawful enterprise being thus shown, every act and declaration of each member of the confederacy, in pursuance of the original concerted plan, and with reference to the common object, is, in contemplation of law, the act and declaration of them all; and is, therefore, original evidence against each of them.[2]

On the trial of an indictment against a physician for administering ergot, with intent to procure a miscarriage, whereby the woman died, evidence, that the defendant was in the habit of receiving patients at his house for medical treatment, and that two young women, inmates of his family, were in the habit of attending them under the defendant's direction, and of carrying them their meals, and that they both so attended the woman whose death was alleged in the

[1] The State *v.* Howard, 32 Vermont, 380 (1859).

[2] Taylor Ev. I. § 527, 3d ed. Purcell Crim. Pl. 290. Commonwealth *v.* Brown, 14 Gray, 419 (1860). In Rex *v.* M'Kenna, Irish Cir. Rep. 461 (1840), Pennefather C.J. thus stated the law: "It is necessary to prove the existence of a conspiracy, and to connect the prisoner with it in the first instance, where you seek to give, in evidence against him, the declaration of a conspirator; and, having done so, you are then at liberty to give, in evidence against the prisoner, acts done by any of the parties whom you have connected with the conspiracy; but when a party's own declarations are to be given in evidence, such preliminary proof is not requisite, and you may, as in other offence, prove the whole case against him by his own admissions."

indictment, and did her chamber-work, and under the defendant's directions administered her medicines and gave her food; that they were present when the child was born, and told the defendant that they had got rid of her child, and that, after her death, the defendant directed them to say they gave her opium and camphor, not opium and calomel, and to say nothing about the ergot; and that he urged them to leave the house, which they did, — is sufficient proof of a common purpose, to render evidence of other acts and declarations of the same persons, not in the defendant's presence, tending to show that they gave ergot to her, admissible against him, with instructions that it is to affect the defendant only, if the jury should be satisfied that the parties had a common purpose and design, and that the acts and declarations were done and made in pursuance thereof.[1]

In the trial of an indictment for murder by poison, in which one count alleges that the deceased was pregnant, and was induced to take the poison by assurances of the defendant that it was a medicinal preparation which would produce a miscarriage, evidence of a conversation two or three years before the time of the acts charged, in which the defendant applied to a witness for information upon the subject of procuring abortions, is inadmissible.[2]

If a medical witness on cross-examination has identified certain medical advertisements as his, they may be read to the jury as a portion of the cross-examination, for the purpose of affecting his credit; but the newspaper in which they are contained cannot be laid before the jury.[3]

In criminal cases, the opinions of medical men of science are very frequently employed as evidence. A physician who has not seen the patient, may, after hearing the evidence of others, be called to prove, on his oath, the general

[1] Commonwealth *v.* Brown, 14 Gray, 419 (1860).
[2] Commonwealth *v.* Hersey, 2 Allen, 173 (1861).
[3] Commonwealth *v.* Hersey, 2 Allen, 173 (1861).

effect of the disease described by them, and its probable consequences in the particular case. The testimony of medical men is constantly admitted with respect to the cause of disease, or of death, in order to connect them with particular acts, and as to the general sane or insane state of the mind of the patient, as collected from a number of circumstances. Such opinions are admissible in evidence, although the professional witnesses found them entirely on the facts, circumstances, and symptoms established by others, and without being personally acquainted with the facts. Thus, in prosecutions for murder, medical men have been allowed to state their opinion, whether the wounds described by witnesses were likely to be the cause of death.[1]

An experienced physician, after having made a post-mortem examination of the body of a female, may, as an expert, give his opinion whether she had been pregnant, and describe the appearances of the body which led to that opinion. He may also give his opinion as to what was the cause of her death.[2]

An exception to the rule rejecting hearsay evidence is allowed in the case of *dying declarations*. It is now settled law, both in England and America, that evidence of this description is admissible in no civil case, and, in criminal cases, only in the single instance of *homicide*, "where the death of the deceased is the subject of the charge, and the circumstances of the death are the subject of the dying declaration."[3] Thus where a prisoner was indicted for administering drugs to a woman, with intent to procure abortion, her statements in extremis were held to be inadmissible.[4]

1 RUSSELL on Crimes, III. 537.

2 The State *v.* Smith, 32 Maine, 370 (1851).

3 Rex *v.* Mead, 2 B. & C. 608, and 4 D. & R. 120. Regina *v.* Hind, Bell C. C. 253. TAYLOR Ev. I. § 644, 3d ed.

4 Rex *v.* Hutchinson, 2 B. & C. 608, note (1822), per BAYLEY J.

APPENDIX.

APPENDIX.

---

1. *Indictment at common law for an assault and administering, etc., to cause a miscarriage.*[1]

THE jurors etc. upon their oath present, that E. F., late of etc., on etc. with force and arms at etc., in and upon one A. E. the wife of E. F. then and there being big and pregnant with child, did make a violent assault, and that the said E. F. then and on divers other days and times, between that day and the day of the taking of this inquisition, with force and arms, at, etc. aforesaid, knowingly, unlawfully, wilfully, wickedly, maliciously and injuriously, did give and administer, and cause and procure to be given and administered to the said A. E., so being big and pregnant with child as aforesaid, divers deadly, dangerous, unwholesome and pernicious pills, herbs, drugs, potions and mixtures, with intent feloniously, wilfully, and of his the said E. F.'s malice aforethought, to kill and murder the said child, with which the said A. E. was so then big and pregnant as aforesaid, by reason and means whereof, not only the said child, whereof the said A. E. was afterwards delivered, and which, by the providence of God was born alive, became and was rendered weak, sick, diseased and distempered in body, but also the said A. E. as well before as at the time of her said delivery, and for a long time, to wit, for the space of six months then next following, became

[1] 3 CHITTY Crim. Law, 798. From the Crown Office Mich. T. 42 Geo. III. See ante, p. 160.

and was rendered weak, sick, diseased and distempered in body, and during all that time, underwent and suffered great and excruciating pains, anguish and torture, both of body and mind, and other wrongs to the said A. E., the said E. F. then and there unlawfully, wilfully, wickedly, maliciously and injuriously did to the grievous damage of the said A. E., and against the peace of etc.

And the jurors, etc. do further present, that the said E. F. afterwards, to wit, on the said etc. with force and arms, at, etc. aforesaid, in and upon the said A. E. then and there being big and pregnant with a certain other child, did make another violent assault, and that the said E. F. then and on divers other days and times, between that day and the day of the taking of this inquisition, with force and arms, at, etc. aforesaid, knowingly, unlawfully, wilfully, wickedly, maliciously and injuriously, did give and administer, and cause and procure to be given and administered to the said A. E., so being big and pregnant with child as last aforesaid, divers other deadly, dangerous, unwholesome and pernicious pills, herbs, drugs, potions and mixtures, by reason and means whereof, etc. *as before.*

And the jurors, etc. do further present that the said E. F. afterwards, to wit, on the said, etc. with force and arms, at, etc. aforesaid, in and upon the said A. E. then and there being big and pregnant with a certain other child, did make another violent assault; and that the said E. F. then and on divers other days and times between that day and the day of the taking of this inquisition, with force and arms, at, etc. aforesaid, knowingly, unlawfully, wilfully, wickedly, maliciously and injuriously, did give and administer, and cause and procure to be given and administered to the said A. E. so being big and pregnant with child as last aforesaid, divers other deadly, dangerous, unwholesome and pernicious pills, herbs, drugs, potions and mixtures, with a wicked intent to cause and procure the said A. E. to miscarry and to bring forth the said last mentioned child, with which she was so big and pregnant as last aforesaid, dead, by reason and means whereof, the said A. E. became and was rendered weak, sick, diseased and distempered in body, and remained and continued so weak, sick, diseased and distempered in body for a long time, to wit, for the space of six months then next following, and during all the time last mentioned underwent and suffered great and excruciating pains, anguish and torture, both of body and mind; and other wrongs to the said A. E., the said E. F. then and there unlawfully, wilfully, wickedly, maliciously and injuriously did, to the grievous damage of the said A. E. and against the peace, etc.

And the jurors, etc. do further present, that the said E. F. afterwards, to wit, on etc. at etc. in and upon the said A. E. then and there being big and pregnant with a certain other child, did make another violent assault, and the said A. E. then and there did violently beat, bruise, wound and ill treat, so that her life was thereby greatly despaired of, and then and there violently, wickedly, and inhumanly, pinched and bruised the belly and private parts of the said A. E., and a certain instrument called a rule, which the said E. F. in his right hand then and there had and held, up and into the womb and body of the said A. E., then and there violently, wickedly and inhumanly, did force and thrust with a wicked intent to cause and procure the said A. E. to miscarry and to bring forth the said child, of which she was so big and pregnant, as last aforesaid, dead, by reason and means of which last mentioned premises, the said A. E. became and was rendered weak, sick, sore, lame, diseased and disordered in body, and remained and continued so weak, sick, sore, lame, diseased and disordered in body, as last aforesaid, for a long time, to wit, for the space of six months then next following, and during all the time last aforesaid, underwent and suffered great and excruciating pains, anguish and torture, both of body and mind, and other wrongs to the said A. E. the said E. F.

then and there unlawfully, wilfully, wickedly, maliciously and injuriously did; to the grievous damage of the said A. E., and against the peace of, etc.

Fifth count for common assault.

2. *For murder by causing premature birth.*[1]

The jurors, etc., upon their oath present, that before and at the time of the committing of the felony and murder hereinafter next mentioned, one Sarah Henson was then quick with a certain male child; and that Ann, the wife of Joseph West, late of, etc., well knowing the said Sarah Henson to be quick with the said male child as aforesaid, and feloniously, wilfully, and of her malice aforethought, devising, contriving, and intending, feloniously, unlawfully, wickedly, and wilfully to cause and procure the said Sarah Henson to bring forth from and out of her womb the said male child, with which she was so quick as aforesaid, and to cause and procure the said male child to be prematurely brought forth from and out of the womb of the said Sarah Henson, and thereby, and by means thereof, the said male child, feloniously, wilfully, and of her malice aforethought, to kill and murder, on, etc., with force and arms, at, etc., in and upon the said male child so quick in the womb of the said Sarah Henson as aforesaid then and there being, feloniously, wilfully, and of her malice aforethought, did make an assault, and that the said Ann West then and there feloniously, wilfully, and of her malice aforethought, did put, place, and force the right hand of the said Ann West into the private parts of the said Sarah Henson, and upward into the womb of the said Sarah Henson, and a certain pin into the private parts, and up into the womb of the said Sarah Henson then and there feloniously, wilfully, and of her malice aforethought, did put, place, and force, and the said Ann West, by such putting, placing, and for-

[1] Regina *v.* West, 2 C. & K. 784, and 2 Cox C. C. 500 (1848), ante, p. 155.

cing the right hand of the said Ann West into the private parts of the said Sarah Henson as aforesaid, and up and into the womb of the said Sarah Henson as aforesaid, and by such putting, placing, and forcing the said pin into the private parts, and up into the womb of the said Sarah Henson as aforesaid, the said Ann West, afterwards, to wit, on, etc., with force and arms, at, etc., feloniously, wilfully, and of her malice aforethought, did cause and procure the said Sarah Henson to bring forth the said male child from and out of the womb of the said Sarah Henson as aforesaid, and did then and there feloniously, wilfully, and of her malice aforethought, cause and procure the said male child to be prematurely born and brought forth alive from and out of the womb of the said Sarah Henson as aforesaid, and that the said male child, by means of being so prematurely born and brought forth alive from and out of the womb of the said Sarah Henson as aforesaid, then and there became and was mortally weakened, debilitated, and emaciated in his body, of which said mortal weakness, debility, and emaciation of the body of the said male child, the said male child for the space of five hours, on, etc., at, etc., did languish, and languishing did live, and then, to wit, on the said last mentioned day, in the year aforesaid, the said male child, at, etc., of the said mortal weakness, debility, and emaciation of his body aforesaid, did die. And so the jurors aforesaid, upon their oath aforesaid, do say, that the said Ann West, the said male child, then and there in manner and form aforesaid, feloniously, wilfully, and of her malice aforethought, did kill and murder; against the peace, etc.

There were three other counts, in two of which the statement of an assault upon the child was omitted.

www.ingramcontent.com/pod-product-compliance
Lightning Source LLC
Chambersburg PA
CBHW031429270326
41930CB00007B/634

* 9 7 8 1 6 1 6 1 9 2 6 7 9 *